Mr. Dryden

The Works of Virgil

Volume I.

Mr. Dryden

The Works of Virgil
Volume I.

ISBN/EAN: 9783742813275

Manufactured in Europe, USA, Canada, Australia, Japa

Cover: Foto ©Andreas Hilbeck / pixelio.de

Manufactured and distributed by brebook publishing software (www.brebook.com)

Mr. Dryden

The Works of Virgil

THE WORKS OF VIRGIL:

TRANSLATED INTO

ENGLISH VERSE

By Mr. DRYDEN.

VOLUME the FIRST.

LONDON:

Printed for C. BATHURST, J. RIVINGTON and Sons, T. CASLON, J. ROBSON, B. LAW, G. ROBINSON, T. CADELL, J. JOHNSON, J. MURRAY, R. BALDWIN, J. DEBRETT, W. FLEXNEY, T. EVANS, and J. MACQUEEN.

MDCCLXXXII.

To the Right Honourable

HUGH Lord CLIFFORD,

Baron of CHUDLEIGH.

My Lord,

I Have found it not more difficult to translate Virgil, than to find such patrons as I desire for my translation. For though England is not wanting in a learned nobility, yet such are my unhappy circumstances, that they have confined me to a narrow choice. To the greater part, I have not the honour to be known; and to some of them I cannot shew at present, by any public act, that grateful respect which I shall ever bear them in my heart. Yet I have no reason to complain of fortune, since in the midst of that abundance I could not possibly have chosen better, than the worthy son of so illustrious a father. He was the patron of my manhood, when I flourished in the opinion of the world; though with small advantage to my fortune, till he awakened the remembrance of my royal master. He was that Pollio, or that Varus, who introduced me to Augustus: And tho' he soon difmiffed himfelf from ftate-affairs, yet in the fhort time of his adminiftration he fhone fo powerfully upon me, that, like the heat of a Ruffian fummer, he ripened the fruits of poetry in a cold climate; and gave me wherewithal to fubfift at leaft, in the long winter which fucceeded. What I now offer to your Lordfhip is the wretched remainder of a fickly age, worn out with ftudy, and oppreffed by fortune: without other fupport than the constancy and patience of a Christian. You, my Lord, are yet in the flower of your youth, and may live to enjoy the benefits of the peace which is promised Europe: I can only hear of that blessing: For years, and, above all things, want of health, have shut me out from sharing in the happiness. The poets, who condemn their Tantalus to hell, had added to his torments, if they had placed him in Elysium, which is the proper emblem of my condition. The fruit and the water may reach my lips, but cannot enter: And if they could, yet I want a palate as well as a digestion. But it is some kind of plea-

DEDICATION.

sure to me, to please those whom I respect. And I am not altogether out of hope, that these Pastorals of Virgil may give your Lordship some delight, though made English by one, who scarce remembers that passion which inspired my author when he wrote them. These were his first essay in poetry, (if the Ceiris was not his;) And it was more excusable in him to describe love when he was young, than for me to translate him when I am old. He died at the age of fifty-two, and I began this work in my great Climacteric. But having perhaps a better constitution than my Author,

I have wronged him less, considering my circumstances, than those who have attempted him before, either in our own, or any modern language. And though this version is not void of errors, yet it comforts me that the faults of others are not worth finding. Mine are neither gross nor frequent, in those Eclogues, wherein my master has raised himself above that humble stile in which Pastoral delights, and which I must confess is proper to the education and converse of Shepherds: For he found the strength of his genius betimes, and was even in his youth preluding to his Georgics, and his Æneis. He could not forbear to

DEDICATION.

try his wings, though his pinions were not hardened to maintain a long laborious flight. Yet sometimes they bore him to a pitch as lofty, as ever he was able to reach afterwards. But when he was admonished by his subject to descend, he came down gently circling in the air, and singing to the ground. Like a lark, melodious in her mounting, and continuing her song till she alights: still preparing for a higher flight at her next sally, and tuning her voice to better music. The fourth, the sixth, and the eighth Pastorals, are clear evidences of this truth. In the three first he contains himself within his bounds; but addressing to Pollio, his great patron, and himself no vulgar poet, he no longer could restrain the freedom of his spirit, but began to assert his native character, which is sublimity. Putting himself under the conduct of the same Cumæan Sybil, whom afterwards he gave for a guide to his Æneas. It is true he was sensible of his own boldness; and we know it by the Paulo Majora, which begins his fourth Eclogue. He remembered, like young Manlius, that he was forbidden to engage; but what avails an express command to a youthful courage which presages victory in the attempt? Encouraged with success, he proceeds farther in the sixth, and invades the province of Philosophy. And notwithstanding that Phœbus had forwarned him of singing wars, as he there confesses, yet he presumed that the search of nature was as free to him as to Lucretius, who at his age explained it according to the principles of Epicurus. In his eighth Eclogue, he has innovated nothing; the former part of it being the complaint and despair of a forsaken lover: the latter a charm of an enchantress, to renew a lost affection. But the complaint perhaps contains some topics which are above the condition of his persons; and our author seems to have made his herdsmen somewhat too learned for their profession: the charms are also of the same nature, but both were copied from Theocritus, and had received the applause of former ages in their original. There is a kind of rusticity in all those pompous verses; somewhat of a holiday shepherd strutting in his country buskins. The like may be observed, both in the Pollio, and the Silenus; where the similitudes are drawn from the woods and meadows. They seem to me to represent our poet betwixt a farmer, and a courtier, when he left Mantua for Rome, and dressed himself in his best habit to appear before his patron: Somewhat too fine for the place from whence he came, and yet retaining part of

DEDICATION.

its simplicity. In the ninth Pastoral he collects some beautiful passages, which were scattered in Theocritus, which he could not insert into any of his former Eclogues, and yet was unwilling they should be lost. In all the rest he is equal to his Sicilian master, and observes like him a just decorum, both of the subject, and the persons. As particularly in the third pastoral, where one of his shepherds describes a bowl, or mazer, curiously carved.

In medio duo signa: Conon, et quis fuit alter,
Descripsit radio totum qui gentibus orbem.

He remembers only the name of Conon, and forgets the other on set purpose: (Whether he means

Aniximander or Eudoxus I difpute not) but he was certainly forgotten, to fhew his country fwain was no great fcholar.

After all, I muft confefs that the boorifh dialect of Theocritus has a fecret charm in it, which the Roman language cannot imitate, tho' Virgil has drawn it down as low as poffibly he could: As in the Cujum Pecus, and fome other words, for which he was fo unjuftly blamed by the bad critics of his age, who could not fee the beauties of that Merum Rus, which the poet defcribed in thofe expreffions. But Theocritus may juftly be preferred as the original, without injury to Virgil, who modeftly contents himself with the second place, and glories only in being the first who transplanted Pastoral into his own country; and brought it there to bear as happily as the cherry-trees which Lucullus brought from Pontus.

Our own Nation has produced a third poet in this kind, not inferior to the two former. For the Shepherd's Kalendar of Spencer is not to be matched in any modern language. Not even by Tasso's Amynta, which infinitely transcends Guarini's Pastor Fido, as having more of nature in it, and being almost wholly clear from the wretched affectation of learning. I will say nothing of the Piscatory

DEDICATION.

Eclogues, because no modern Latin can bear criticism. It is no wonder that rolling down through so many barbarous ages, from the spring of Virgil, it bears along with it the filth and ordures of the Goths and Vandals. Neither will I mention Monsieur Fontenelle, the living glory of the French. It is enough for him to have excelled his master Lucian, without attempting to compare our miserable age with that of Virgil, or Theocritus. Let me only add, for his reputation,

——— Si Pergama dextrâ
Defendi possent, etiam hâc defensa fuissent.

But Spencer being master of our northern dialect, and skilled in Chaucer's English, has so exactly imitated the Doric of Theocritus, that his love is a perfect image of that passion which God infused into both sexes, before it was corrupted with the knowledge of arts, and the ceremonies of what we call good manners.

My Lord, I know to whom I dedicate: And could not have been induced by any motive to put this part of Virgil, or any other, into unlearned hands. You have read him with pleasure, and I dare say, with admiration, in the Latin, of which you are a master. You have added to your natural endowments, which, without flattery, are eminent, the superstructures of study, and the knowledge of good authors. Courage, probity, and humanity are inherent in you. These virtues have ever been habitual to the ancient house of Cumberland, from whence you are descended, and of which our chronicles make so honourable mention in the long wars betwixt the rival families of York and Lancaster. Your forefathers have asserted the party which they chose till death, and died for its defence in the fields of battle. You have besides the fresh remembrance of your noble father; from whom you never can degenerate.

——— Nec imbellem feroces
Progenerant Aquilæ Columbam.

It being almoſt morally impoſſible for you to be other than you are by kind; I need neither praiſe nor incite your virtue. You are acquainted with the Roman hiſtory, and know without my information, that patronage and clientſhip always deſcended from the fathers to the ſons, and that the ſame plebeian houſes had recourſe to the ſame patrician line, which had formerly protected them; and followed their principles and fortunes to the laſt. So that I am your Lordſhip's by deſcent, and part of your inheritance. And the natural inclination which I have to serve you, adds to your paternal right, for I was wholly yours from the first moment, when I had the happiness and honour of being known to you. Be pleased therefore to accept the Rudiments of Virgil's poetry: Coarsely translated, I confess, but which yet retains some beauties of the author which neither the barbarity of our language, nor my unskilfulness could so much fully, but that they appear sometimes in the dim mirrour which I hold before you. The subject is not unsuitable to your youth, which allows you yet to love, and is proper to your present scene of life. Rural recreations abroad, and books at home, are the innocent pleasures of a man who is early wise, and gives fortune no more hold of him, than of necessity he must. It is good, on some occasions, to think beforehand as little as we can; to enjoy as much of the present as will not endanger our futurity, and to provide ourselves of the Virtuoso's saddle, which will be sure to amble, when the world is upon the hardest trot. What I humbly offer to your Lordship, is of this nature. - I wish it pleasant, and am sure it is innocent. May you ever continue your esteem for Virgil; and not lessen it, for the faults of his translator;

DEDICATION.

who is, with all manner of respect and sense of gratitude,

My Lord,

Your Lordship's

most humble and

most obedient servant,

JOHN DRYDEN.

THE LIFE

OF

PUB. VIRGILIUS MARO.

Written by WILLIAM WALSH, Esq.

VIRGIL was born at Mantua, which city was built no less than three hundred years before Rome; and was the capital of the New Hetruria, as himself, no less antiquary, than poet, assures us. His birth is said to have happened in the first consulship of Pompey the Great, and Lic. Crassus; but since the relater of this presently after contradicts himself, and

Virgil's manner of addressing to Octavius, implies a greater difference of age than that of seven years, as appears by his first Pastoral, and other places; it is reasonable to set the date of it something backwarder: And the writer of his life having no certain memorials to work upon, seems to have pitched upon the two most illustrious consuls he could find about that time, to signalize the birth of so eminent a man. But it is beyond all question, that he was born on, or near, the fifteenth of October. Which day was kept festival in honour to his memory, by the Latin, as the birth-day of Homer was by the Greek poets. And so near a resemblance there is betwixt the lives of these two famous Epic writers, that Virgil seems to have followed the fortune of the other, as well as the subject and manner of his writing. For Homer is said to have been of very mean parents, such as got their bread by daylabour; so is Virgil. Homer is said to be base-born; so is Virgil. The former to have been born in the open air, in a ditch, or by the bank of a river; so is the latter.

VIRGIL.

There was a poplar planted near the place of Virgil's birth, which suddenly grew up to an unusual height and bulk, and to which the superstitious neighbourhood attributed marvellous virtue. Homer had his poplar too, as Herodotus relates, which was visited with great veneration. Homer is described by one of the ancients, to have been of a slovenly and neglected mien and habit, so was Virgil. Both were of a very delicate and sickly constitution: Both addicted to travel, and the study of astrology: Both had their compositions usurped by others: Both envied and traduced during their lives. We know not so much as the true names of either of them with any exactness: for the critics are not yet agreed how the word [Virgil] should be written; and of Homer's name there is no certainty at all. Whosoever shall consider this parallel in so many particulars, (and more might be added) would be inclined to think, that either the same stars ruled strongly at the nativities of them both; or, what is a great deal more probable, that the Latin grammarians wanting materials for the former part of Virgil's life, after the legendary fashion, supplied it out of Herodotus; and, like ill face-painters, not being able to hit the true features, endeavoured to make amends by a great deal of impertinent landscape and drapery.

Without troubling the reader with needless quotations, now, or afterwards; the most probable opinion is, that Virgil was the son of a servant, or assistant to a wandering astrologer, who practised physic. For Medicus, Magus, as Juvenal observes, usually went together; and this course of life was followed by a great many Greeks and Syrians; of one of which nation it seems not improbable, that Virgil's father was. Nor could a man of that profession have chosen a fitter place to settle in, than that most superstitious tract of Italy; which by her ridiculous rites and ceremonies as much enslaved the Romans, as the Romans did the Hetrurians by their arms. This man therefore having got together some money, which stock he improved by his skill in planting and husbandry, had the good fortune, at last, to marry his mas-

ter's daughter, by whom he had Virgil;
and this woman seems, by her mother's
side, to have been of good extraction; for
she was nearly related to Quintilius Varus,
whom Paterculus, assures us to have been
of an illustrious, though not patrician family; and there is honourable mention
made of it in the history of the second
Carthaginian war. It is certain, that they
gave him very good education, to which
they were inclined, not so much by the
dreams of his mother, and those presages
which Donatus relates, as by the early in-
dications which he gave of a sweet disposition, and excellent wit. He passed the
first seven years of his life at Mantua, not
seventeen, as Scaliger miscorrects his author; for the initia ætatis can hardly be
supposed to extend so far. From thence
he removed to Cremona, a noble Roman colony; and afterwards to Milan. In all which
places he prosecuted his studies with great
application; he read over all the best Latin and Greek authors, for which he had
convenience by the no remote distance of
Marseilles, that famous Greek colony,

which maintained its politeness, and purity of language, in the midſt of all thoſe barbarous nations amongſt which it was ſeated: and ſome tincture of the latter ſeems to have deſcended from them down to the modern French. He frequented the moſt eminent profeſſors of the Epicurean philoſophy, which was then much in vogue, and will be always, in declining and ſickly ſtates. But finding no ſatisfactory account from his maſter Syron, he paſſed over to the Academic ſchool, to which he adhered the reſt of his life, and deſerved, from a great emperor, the title of the Plato of Poets. He compoſed at leiſure hours a great number of verſes on various ſubjects; and deſirous rather of a great than early fame, he permitted his kinſman, and fellow-ſtudent Varus, to derive the honour of one of his tragedies to himſelf. Glory neglected in proper time and place, returns often with large increaſe, and ſo he found it: For Varus afterwards proved a great inſtrument of his riſe. In ſhort, it was here that he formed the plan, and collected the materials of all those excellent pieces which he afterwards finished, or was forced to leave less perfect by his death. But whether it were the unwholesomeness of his native air, of which he somewhere complains, or his too great abstinence, and night-watchings at his study, to which he was always addicted, as Augustus observes; or possibly the hopes of improving himself by travel, he resolved to remove to the most southern tract of Italy; and it was hardly possible for him not to take Rome in his way; as is evident to any one who shall cast an eye on the map of Italy: and therefore the late French editor of his works is mistaken, when he asserts that he never saw Rome, till he came to petition for his estate. He gained the acquaintance of the master of the horse to Octavius; and cured a great many diseases of horses, by methods they had never heard of. It fell out, at the same time, that a very fine colt, which promised great strength and speed, was presented to Octavius: Virgil assured them, that he came of a faulty mare, and would prove a jade;

upon trial it was found as he had said: his judgment proved right in several other instances, which was the more surprising, because the Romans knew least of natural causes of any civilized nation in the world: And those meteors and prodigies, which cost them incredible sums to expiate, might easily have been accounted for, by no very profound naturalist. It is no wonder, therefore, that Virgil was in so great reputation, as to be at last introduced to Octavius himself. That prince was then at variance with Marc Antony, who vexed him with a great many libelling letters, in which he reproaches him with the baseness of his parentage, that he came of a scrivener, a ropemaker, and a baker, as Suetonius tells us. Octavius finding that Virgil had passed so exact a judgment upon the breed of dogs and horses, thought that he possibly might be able to give him some light concerning his own. He took him into his closet, where they continued in private a considerable time. Virgil, was a great mathematician, which, in the sense of those times, took in astrology: and if there be any thing in that art, which I can hardly believe; if that be true which the ingenious De la Chambre asserts confidently, that from the marks on the body, the configuration of the planets at a nativity may be gathered, and the marks might be told by knowing the nativity, never had one of those artists a fairer opportunity to shew his skill, than Virgil now had; for Octavius had moles upon his body, exactly resembling the constellation called Ursa Major. But Virgil had other helps: the predictions of Cicero, and Catullus, and that vote of the senate had gone abroad, that no child born at Rome, in the year of his nativity, should be bred up; because the seers assured them that an emperor was born that year. Besides this, Virgil had heard of the Assyrian, and Egyptian prophecies (which, in truth, were no other but the Jewish,) that about that time a great king was to come into the world. Himself takes notice of them, Æn. VI. where he uses a very significant word (now in all liturgies) hujus in adventu, so in another place, adventu propiore Dei.

> At his foreseen approach already quake
> Assyrian kingdoms, and Mœotis' lake.
> Nile hears him knocking at his seven-fold gates——

Every one knows whence this was taken: it was rather a mistake, than impiety in Virgil, to apply these prophecies, which belonged to the Saviour of the world, to the person of Octavius, it being a usual piece of flattery for near a hundred years together, to attribute them to their emperors, and other great men. Upon the whole matter, it is very probable, that Virgil predicted to him the empire at this time. And it will appear yet the more, if we consider that he assures him of his being received into the number of the Gods, in his first Pastoral, long before the thing came to pass; which prediction seems grounded upon his former mistake. This was a secret, not to be divulged at that time, and therefore it is no wonder that the slight story in Donatus was given abroad to palliate the matter. But certain it is, that Octavius dismissed him with great marks of esteem, and earnestly recommended the protection of Virgil's affairs to Pollio, then lieutenant of the Cis-Alpine Gaul, where Virgil's patrimony lay. This Pollio, from a mean original, became one of the most considerable persons of his time: a good general, orator, statesman, historian, poet, and favourer of learned men; above all, he was a man of honour in those critical times. He had joined with Octavius and Antony, in revenging the barbarous assassination of Julius Cæsar: when they two were at variance, he would neither follow Antony, whose courses he detested, nor join with Octavius against him, out of a grateful sense of some former obligations. Augustus, who thought it his interest to oblige men of principles, notwithstanding this, received him afterwards into favour, and promoted him to the highest honours. And thus much I thought fit to say of Pollio, because he was one of Virgil's greatest friends. Being therefore eased of domestic cares, he pursues his journey to Naples: The charming situation of that place, and view of the beautiful villas of the Roman nobility, equalling the magnificence of the greatest kings; the neighbourhood of the Baiæ, whither the sick resorted for recovery, and the statesman when he was politicly sick, whither the wanton went for pleasure, and witty men for good company; the wholsomness of the air, and improving conversation, the best air of all, contributed not only to the re-establishing his health, but to the forming of his stile, and rendering him master of that happy turn of verse, in which he much surpasses all the Latins, and, in a less advantageous language, equals even Homer himself. He proposed to use his talent in poetry, only for scaffolding to build a convenient fortune, that he might prosecute with less interruption, those nobler studies to which his elevated genius led him, and which he describes in these admirable lines:

> Me vero primùm dulces ante omnia musæ,
> Quarum sacra fero ingenti perculsus amore,
> Accipiant, cœlique vias et sidera monstrent,
> Defectus solis varios, lunæque labores;
> Unde tremor terris, &c.

But the current of that martial age, by some strange antiperistasis, drove so violently towards poetry, that he was at last carried down with the stream. For not only the young nobility, but Octavius, and Pollio, Cicero in his old age, Julius Cæsar, and the stoical Brutus, a little before, would needs be tampering with the Muses, the two latter had taken great care to have their poems curiously bound, and lodged in the most famous libraries; but neither the sacredness of those places, nor the greatness of their names, could preserve ill poetry. Quitting therefore the study of the law, after having pleaded but one cause with indifferent success, he resolved to push his fortune this way, which he seems to have discontinued for some time, and that may be the reason why the Culex, his first pastoral, now extant, has little besides the novelty of the subject, and the moral of the fable, which contains an exhortation to gratitude, to recommend it; had it been as correct as his other pieces, nothing more proper and pertinent could have at that time been addressed to the young Octavius: for the year in which he presented it, probably at the Baiæ, seems to be the very same, in which that prince consented (though with seeming reluctance) to the death of Cicero, under whose consulship he was born, the preserver of his life, and chief instrument of his advancement. There is no reason to question its being genuine, as the late French editor does; its meanness, in comparison of Virgil's other works, (which is that writer's only objection) confutes himself: for Martial, who certainly saw the true copy, speaks of it with contempt; and yet that Pastoral equals at least the address to the Dauphin, which is prefixed to the late edition. Octavius, to unbend his mind from application to public business, took frequent turns to Baiæ, and Sicily; where he composed his poem called Sicelides, which Virgil seems to allude to, in the Pastoral beginning Sicelides Musæ; this gave him opportunity of refreshing that prince's memory of him, and about that time he wrote his Ætna. Soon after he seems to have made a voyage to Athens, and at his return presented his Ceiris, a more elaborate piece, to the noble and eloquent Meſſala. The forementioned author groundlesly taxes this as suppoſititious: for besides other critical marks, there are no leſs than fifty or sixty verſes, altered, indeed and poliſhed, which he inſerted in the Paſtorals, according to his faſhion; and from thence they were called Eclogues, or ſelect Bucolics. We thought fit to uſe a title more intelligible, the reaſon of the other being ceaſed; and we are ſupported by Virgil's own authority, who expreſly calls them Carmina Paſtorum. The French editor is again miſtaken, in aſſerting, that the Ceiris is borrowed from the ninth of Ovid's Metamorphoſis: he might have more reaſonably conjectured it to be taken from Parthenius, the Greek poet, from whom Ovid borrowed a great part of his work. But it is indeed taken from neither, but from that learned, unfortunate poet, Apollonius Rhodius, to whom Virgil is more indebted than to any other Greek writer, excepting Homer. The reader will be ſatisfied of this, if he conſults that author in his own language, for the tranflation is a great deal more obfcure than the original.

Whilft Virgil thus enjoyed the fweets of a learned privacy, the troubles of Italy cut off his little fubfiftence; but by a ftrange turn of human affairs, which ought to keep good men from ever defpairing, the lofs of his eftate proved the effectual way of making his fortune. The occafion of it was this; Octavius, as himfelf relates, when he was but nineteen years of age, by a mafterly ftroke of policy, had gained the veteran legions into his fervice, (and by that ftep, outwitted all the republican fenate.) They grew now very clamorous for their pay: the treafury being exhaufted, he was forced to make affignment upon lands, and none but in Italy itfelf would content them. He pitched upon Cremona as the moft diftant from Rome; but that not fufficing, he afterwards threw in part of the ftate of Mantua. Cremona was a rich and noble colony, fettled a little before the invafion of Hannibal. During that tedious and bloody war, they had done several important services to the commonwealth. And when eighteen other colonies, pleading poverty and depopulation, refused to contribute money, or to raise recruits, they of Cremona voluntarily paid a double quota of both. But past services are a fruitless plea; civil wars are one continued act of ingratitude: in vain did the miserable mothers, with their famishing infants in their arms, fill the streets with their numbers, and the air with lamentations; the craving legions were to be satisfied at any rate. Virgil, involved in the common calamity, had recourse to his old patron Pollio; but he was, at this time, under a cloud; however, compassionating so worthy a man, not of a make to struggle through the world, he did what he could, and recommended him to Mecænas, with whom he still kept a private correspondence. The name of this great man being much better known than one part of his character, the reader, I presume, will not be displeased if I supply it in this place.

 Though he was of as deep reach, and

easy dispatch of business as any in his time, yet he designedly lived beneath his true character. Men had oftentimes meddled in public affairs, that they might have more ability to furnish for their pleasures: Mecænas, by the honestest hypocrisy that ever was, pretended to a life of pleasure, that he might render more effectual service to his master. He seemed wholly to amuse himself with the diversions of the town, but under that mask was the greatest minister of his age. He would be carried in a careless, effeminate posture through the streets in his chair, even to the degree of a proverb, and yet there was not a cabal of ill disposed persons which he had not early notice of; and that too in a city as large as London and Paris, and perhaps two or three more of the most populous put together. No man better understood that art so necessary to the great; the art of declining envy: being but of a gentleman's family, not Patrician, he would not provoke the nobility by accepting invidious honours; but wisely satisfied himself that he had the ear of Augustus, and the secret of the empire. He seems to have committed but one great fault, which was the trusting a secret of high consequence to his wife; but his master, en ugh uxorious himself, made his own frailty more excusable by generously forgiving that of his favourite. He kept in all his greatness exact measures with his friends; and chusing them wisely, found by experience, that good sense and gratitude are almost inseparable. This appears in Virgil and Horace; the former, besides the honour he did him to all posterity, returned his liberalities at his death: The other, whom Mecænas recommended with his last breath, was too generous to stay behind, and enjoy the favour of Augustus: he only desired a place in his tomb, and to mingle his ashes with those of his deceased benefactor. But this was seventeen hundred years ago. Virgil, thus powerfully supported, thought it mean to petition for himself alone, but resolutely solicits the cause of his whole country, and seems, at first, to have met with some encouragement: but the matter cooling, he was forced to sit down contented with the grant of his own estate. He goes therefore to Mantua, produces his warrant to a captain of foot, whom he found in his house. Arrius who had eleven points of the law, and fierce of the services he had rendered to Octavius, was so far from yielding possession, that words growing betwixt them, he wounded him dangerously, forced him to fly, and at last to swim the river Mincius to save his life. Virgil, who used to say, that no virtue was so necessary as patience, was forced to drag a sick body half the length of Italy, back again to Rome, and by the way, probably, composed his ninth Pastoral, which may seem to have been made up in haste out of the fragments of some other pieces; and naturally enough represents the disorder of the poet's mind, by its disjointed fashion, though there be another reason to be given elsewhere of its want of connection. He handsomely states his case in that poem, and with the pardonable resentments of injured innocence, not only claims Octavius's promise, but hints to him the uncertainty of human greatness and glory: all was taken in good part by that wife prince. At laſt effectual orders were given. About this time, he compoſed that admirable poem, which is ſet firſt, out of reſpect to Cæſar; for he does not ſeem either to have had leiſure, or to have been in the humour of making ſo ſolemn an acknowledgment, till he was poſſeſſed of the benefit. And now he was in ſo great reputation and intereſt, that he reſolved to give up his land to his parents, and himſelf to the court. His paſtorals were in ſuch eſteem, that Pollio, now again in high favour with Cæſar, deſired him to reduce them into a volume. Some modern writer that has a conſtant flux of verſe, would ſtand amazed how Virgil could employ three whole years in reviſing five or ſix hundred verſes, moſt of which, probably, were made ſome time before; but there is more reaſon to wonder how he could do it ſo ſoon in ſuch perfection. A coarſe ſtone is preſently faſhioned; but a diamond of not many carats, is many weeks in ſawing, and in poliſhing many more. He who put Virgil upon this, had a politic good end in it.

The continued civil wars had laid Italy almost waste; the ground was uncultivated and unstocked; upon which ensued such a famine, and insurrection, that Cæsar hardly escaped being stoned at Rome; his ambition being looked upon by all parties as the principal occasion of it. He set himself therefore with great industry to promote country improvements; and Virgil was serviceable to his design, as the good keeper of the bees, Geor. iv.

Tinnitúsque cie, et matris quate cymbala circum,
Ipsiæ confident——

That emperor afterwards thought it matter worthy a public inscription

Rediit cultus agris.

Which seems to be the motive that induced Mecænas, to put him upon writing his Georgics, or books of husbandry; a design as new in Latin verse, as Pastorals, before Virgil were in Italy; which work took up seven of the most vigorous years of his life, for he was now at least thirty-four years of age; and here Virgil shines in his meridian. A great part of this work seems to have been rough-drawn before he left Mantua, for an ancient writer has observed, that the rules of husbandry laid down in it, are better calculated for the soil of Mantua, than for the more sunny climate of Naples, near which place, and in Sicily, he finished it. But lest his genius should be depressed by apprehensions of want, he had a good estate settled upon him, and a house in the pleasantest part of Rome; the principal furniture of which was a well-chosen library, which stood open to all comers of learning and merit: and what recommended the situation of it most, was the neighbourhod of his Mecænas; and thus he could either visit Rome, or return to his privacy at Naples, through a pleasant road adorned on each side with pieces of antiquity, of which he was so great a lover, and in the intervals of them seemed almost one continued street of three days journey.

THE LIFE OF

Cæsar having now vanquished Sextus Pompeius, a spring-tide of prosperities breaking in upon him, before he was ready to receive them as he ought, fell sick of the imperial evil, the desire of being thought something more than man. Ambition is an infinite folly: when it has attained to the utmost pitch of human greatness, it soon falls to making pretensions upon heaven. The crafty Livia would needs be drawn in the habit of a priestess by the shrine of the new God: and this became a fashion not to be dispensed with amongst the ladies: the devotion was wondrous great amongst the Romans, for it was their interest, and, which sometimes avails more, it was the mode. Virgil, though he despised the heathen superstitions, and is so bold as to call Saturn and Janus by no better a name than that of old men, and might deserve the title of subverter of superstitions, as well as Varro, thought fit to follow the maxim of Plato his master, that every one should serve the Gods after the usage of his own country; and therefore was not the last to present his incense, which was of too rich a compofition for fuch an altar: and by his addrefs to Cæfar on this occafion, made an unhappy precedent to Lucan and other poets which came after him, Geor. i. and iii. And this poem being now in great forwardnefs, Cæfar, who, in imitation of his predeceffor Julius, never intermitted his ftudies in the camp, and much lefs in other places, refrefhing himfelf by a fhort ftay in a pleafant village of Campania, would needs be entertained with the rehearfal of fome part of it. Virgil recited with a marvellous grace, and fweet accent of voice, but his lungs failing him, Mecænas himfelf fupplied his place for what remained. Such a piece of condefcenfion would now be very furprifing, but it was no more than cuftomary amongft friends, when learning paffed for quality. Lelius, the fecond man of Rome in his time, had done as much for that poet, out of whofe drofs Virgil would fometimes pick gold; as himfelf faid, when one found him reading Ennius: (the like he did by fome verfes of Varro and Pacuvius, Lucretius and Cicero, which he inferted into his works.) But learned men then lived easy and familiarly with the great: Augustus himself would sometimes sit down betwixt Virgil and Horace, and say, jestingly, that he sate betwixt sighing and tears, alluding to the asthma of one, and rheumatic eyes of the other; he would frequently correspond with them, and never leave a letter of theirs unanswered: nor were they under the constraint of formal superscriptions in the beginning, nor of violent superlatives at the close of their letters: the invention of these is a modern refinement. In which this may be remarked, in passing, that (humble servant) is respect, but (friend) an affront, which notwithstanding implies the former, and a great deal more. Nor does true greatness lose by such familiarity; and those who have it not, as Mecænas and Pollio had, are not to be accounted proud, but rather very discreet, in their reserves. Some play-house beauties do wisely to be seen at a distance, and to have the lamps twinkle betwixt them and the spectators.

But now Cæsar, who, though he were none of the greatest soldiers, was certainly the greatest traveller, of a prince, that had ever been, (for which Virgil so dexterously compliments him, Æneid vi.) takes a voyage to Ægypt, and having happily finished the war, reduces that mighty kingdom into the form of a province; over which he appointed Gallus his lieutenant. This is the same person to whom Virgil addresses his tenth Pastoral; changing, in compliance to his request, his purpose of limiting them to the number of the Muses. The praises of this Gallus took up a considerable part of the fourth book of the Georgics, according to the general consent of antiquity: but Cæsar would have it put out, and yet the seam in the poem is still to be discerned; and the matter of Aristeus's recovering his bees, might have been dispatched in less compass, without fetching the causes so far, or interesting so many gods and goddesses in that affair. Perhaps some readers may be inclined to think this, though very much laboured, not the most entertaining part of that work; so hard it is for the greatest masters to paint against their inclination. But Cæsar was contented that he should be mentioned in the last Pastoral, because it might be taken for a satyrical sort of commendation; and the character he there stands under, might help to excuse his cruelty, in putting an old servant to death for no very great crime.

And now having ended, as he begins his Georgics, with solemn mention of Cæsar, an argument of his devotion to him: he begins his Æneis, according to the common account, being now turned of forty. But that work had been, in truth, the subject of much earlier meditation. Whilst he was working upon the first book of it, this passage, so very remarkable in history, fell out, in which Virgil had a great share.

Cæsar, about this time, either cloyed with glory, or terrified by the example of his predecessor, or to gain the credit of moderation with the people, or possibly to feel the pulse of his friends, deliberated whether he should retain the sovereign power, or restore the commonwealth.

VIRGIL.

Agrippa, who was a very honest man, but whose view was of no great extent, advised him to the latter; but Mecænas, who had thoroughly studied his master's temper, in an eloquent oration, gave contrary advice. That emperor was too politic to commit the oversight of Cromwell, in a deliberation something resembling this. Cromwell had never been more desirous of the power than he was afterwards of the title of king: and there was nothing in which the heads of the parties, who were all his creatures, would not comply with him: but by too vehement allegation of arguments against it, he, who had outwitted every body besides, at last out-witted himself, by too deep dissimulation: for his council, thinking to make their court by assenting to his judgment, voted unanimously for him against his inclination; which surprised and troubled him to such a degree, that as soon as he had got into his coach, he fell into a swoon. But Cæsar knew his people better, and his council being thus divided, he asked Virgil's advice. Thus a poet had the honour of determining the greatest point that ever was in debate, betwixt the son-in-law and favourite of Cæsar. Virgil delivered his opinion in words to this effect. "The "change of a popular into an absolute "government, has generally been of very "ill consequence: for betwixt the hatred "of the people, and injustice of the prince, "it of necessity comes to pass that they "live in distrust, and mutual apprehen- "sions. But if the commons knew a just "person, whom they entirely confided in, "it would be for the advantage of all par- "ties, that such a one should be their sove- "reign: wherefore if you should continue to "administer justice impartially, as hitherto "you have done, your power will prove "safe to yourself, and beneficial to man- "kind." This excellent sentence, which seems taken out of Plato, (with whose writings the grammarians were not much acquainted, and therefore cannot reasonably be suspected of forgery in this matter) contains the true state of affairs at that time: for the commonwealth maxims were now no longer practicable; the Romans had only the haughtiness of the old commonwealth left, without one of its virtues. And this sentence we find, almost in the same words, in the first book of the Æneis, which at this time he was writing; and one mig't wonder that none of his commentators have taken notice of it. He compares a tempest to a popular insurrection, as Cicero had compared a sedition to a storm, a little before.

> Ac veluti magno in populo, cum sæpe coorta est
> Seditio, sævitque animis ignobile vulgus,
> Jamque faces, ac saxa volant, furor arma ministrat:
> Tum pietate gravem, et meritis si forte virum quem
> Conspexere silent, arrectisque auribus adstant:
> Ille regit dictis animos, et pectora mulcet.

Piety and merit were the two great virtues which Virgil every where attributes to Augustus, and in which that prince, at least politically, if not so truly, fixed his character, as appears by the Marmor Ancyr, and several of his medals. Freinshemius, the learned supplementor of Livy, has inserted this relation into his history; nor is there any good reason, why Ruæus should account it fabulous. The title of a poet in those days did not abate, but heighten the character of the gravest senator. Virgil was one of the best and wisest men of his time, and in so popular esteem, that one hundred thousand Romans rose when he came into the theatre, and paid him the same respect they used to Cæsar himself, as Tacitus assures us. And if, Augustus invited Horace to assist him in writing his letters, and every body knows that the Rescripta Imperatorum were the laws of the empire, Virgil might well deserve a place in the cabinet-council.

And now Virgil prosecutes his Æneis, which had anciently the title of the Imperial Poem, or Roman History, and deservedly; for though he were too artful a writer to set down events in exact historical order, for which Lucan is justly blamed; yet are all the most considerable affairs and persons of Rome comprised in this poem. He deduces the history of Italy from before Saturn to the reign of king Latinus; and reckons up the successors of Æneas, who reigned at Alba, for the space of three hundred years, down to the birth of Romulus; describes the persons and principal exploits of all the kings, to their expulsion, and the settling of the commonwealth. After this, he touches promiscuously the most remarkable occurrences at home and abroad, but insists more particularly upon the exploits of Augustus; insomuch that though this assertion may appear, at first, a little surprising, he has in his works deduced the history of a considerable part of the world from its original, through the fabulous and heroic ages, through the monarchy and commonwealth of Rome, for the space of four thousand years, down to within less than forty of our Saviour's time, of whom he has preserved a most illustrious prophecy. Besides this, he points at many remarkable passages of history under feigned names: the destruction of Alba, and Veii, under that of

Troy: the star Venus, which, Varro says, guided Æneas in his voyage to Italy, in that verse,

Matre deâ monstrante viam.

Romulus's lance taking root, and budding, is described in that passage concerning Polydorus, Æneid. iii.

—————— Confixum ferrea texit
Telorum seges, et jaculis increvit acutis.

The stratagem of the Trojans boring holes in their ships, and sinking them, lest the Latins should burn them, under that fable of their being transformed into sea-nymphs: and therefore the ancients had no such reason to condemn that fable as groundless and absurd. Cocles swimming the river Tyber, after the bridge was broken down behind him, is exactly painted in the four last verses of the ninth book, under the character of Turnus. Marius hiding himself in the morass of Minturnæ, under the person of Simon:

Limosoque lacu per noctem obscurus in ulva
Delitui ———

VIRGIL.

Those verses in the second book concerning Priam;

Jacet ingens littore truncus, &c.

seem originally made upon Pompey the Great. He seems to touch the imperious and intriguing humour of the empress Livia, under the character of Juno. The irresolute and weak Lepidus is well represented under the person of king Latinus; Augustus with the character of Pont. Max. under that of Æneas; and the rash courage (always unfortunate in Virgil) of Marc Antony in Turnus; the railing eloquence of Cicero in his Philippics is well imitated in the oration of Drances; the dull faithful Agrippa, under the person of Achates; accordingly this character is flat; Achates kills but one man, and himself receives one slight wound, but neither says nor does any thing very considerable in the whole poem. Curio, who sold his country for about two hundred thousand pounds, is stigmatized in that verse:

"Vendidit hic auro patriam, dominumque potentem
    Impofuit ——

Livy relates that, prefently after the death of the two Scipio's in Spain, when Martius took upon him the command, a blazing meteor fhone around his head, to the aftonifhment of his foldiers: Virgil transfers this to Æneas:

Lætafque vomunt duo tempora flammas.

It is ftrange that the commentators have not taken notice of this. Thus the ill omen which happened a little before the battle of Thrafimen, when fome of the centurions lances took fire miraculoufly, is hinted in the like accident which befel Aceftes, before the burning of the Trojan fleet in Sicily. The reader will eafily find many more fuch inftances. In other writers there is often well covered ignorance; in Virgil, concealed learning.

His filence of fome illuftrious perfons is no lefs worth obfervation. He fays nothing of Scævola, becaufe he attempted to aſſaſſinate a king, though a declared enemy. Nor of the younger Brutus; for he effected what the other endeavoured. Nor of the younger Cato, becauſe he was an implacable enemy of Julius Cæſar; nor could the mention of him be pleaſing to Auguſtus; and that paſſage

His dantem jura Catonem,

may relate to his office, as, he was a very ſevere cenſor. Nor would he name Cicero, when the occaſion of mentioning him came full in his way, when he ſpeaks of Catiline; becauſe he afterwards approved the murder of Cæſar, though the plotters were too wary to truſt the orator with their deſign. Some other poets knew the art of ſpeaking well; but Virgil, beyond this, knew the admirable ſecret of being eloquently ſilent. Whatſoever was moſt curious in Fabius Pictor, Cato the elder, Varro, in the Ægyptian antiquities, in the form of ſacrifice, in the ſolemnities of making peace and war, is preſerved in this poem. Rome is ſtill above ground, and flouriſhing in Virgil. And all this he performs with admirable brevity. The Æneis was once near twenty times bigger than he left it; so that he spent as much time in blotting out, as some moderns have done in writing whole volumes. But not one book has his finishing strokes: the sixth seems one of the most perfect, the which, after long intreaty, and sometimes threats of Augustus, he was at last prevailed upon to recite: this fell out about four years before his own death: that of Marcellus, whom Cæsar designed for his successor, happened a little before this recital: Virgil therefore, with his usual dexterity, inserted his funeral panegyric in those admirable lines, beginning

> O nate, ingentem luctum ne quære tuorum, &c.

His mother, the excellent Octavia, the best wife of the worst husband that ever was, to divert her grief, would be of the auditory. The poet artificially deferred the naming Marcellus, till their passions were raised to the highest; but the mention of it put both her and Augustus into such a passion of weeping, that they commanded him to proceed no further; Virgil answered, that he had already ended that passage. Some relate, that Octavia fainted away; but afterwards she presented the poet with two thousand one hundred pounds, odd money; a round sum for twenty-seven verses. But they were Virgil's. Another writer says, that with a royal magnificence, she ordered him massy plate, unweighed, to a great value.

And now he took up a resolution of travelling into Greece, there to set the last hand to this work; proposing to devote the rest of his life to philosophy, which had been always his principal passion. He justly thought it a foolish figure for a grave man to be overtaken by death, whilst he was weighing the cadence of words, and measuring verses; unless necessity should constrain it, from which he was well secured by the liberality of that learned age. But he was not aware, that whilst he allotted three years for the revising of his poem, he drew bills upon a failing bank: for unhappily meeting August is at Athens, he thought himself obliged to wait upon him into Italy, but being desirous to see all he could of the Greek antiquities, he fell into a languishing distemper at Megara; this neglected at first, proved mortal. The agitation of the vessel, for it was now autumn, near the time of his birth, brought him so low, that he could hardly reach Brindisi. In his sickness he frequently, and with great importunity, called for his scrutore, that he might burn his Æneis; but Augustus interposing by his royal authority, he made his last will, of which something shall be said afterwards. And considering probably how much Homer had been disfigured by the arbitrary compilers of his works, obliged Tucca and Varius to add nothing, nor so much as fill up the breaks he left in his poem. He ordered that his bones should be carried to Naples, in which place he had passed the most agreeable part of his life. Augustus, not only as executor and friend, but according to the duty of the Pont. Max. when a funeral happened in his family, took care himself to see the will punctually executed. He went out of the world with all that calmness of mind with which the ancient writer of his life says he came into it: making the inscription of his monument himself; for he began and ended his poetical compositions with an epitaph. And this he made exactly according to the law of his master Plato on such occasions, without the least ostentation.

I sung flocks, tillage, heroes; Mantua gave
Me life, Brundusium death, Naples a grave.

THE LIFE OF

A SHORT ACCOUNT

OF HIS

Person, Manners and Fortune.

HE was of a very swarthy complexion, which might proceed from the southern extraction of his father; tall and wide shouldered, so that he may be thought to have described himself under the character of Musæus, whom he calls the best of poets.

 ―――Medium nam plurima turba
Hunc habet, atque humeris extantem suspicit
  altis.

His sickliness, studies, and the troubles he met with, turned his hair gray before the ufual time; he had an hefitation in his speech, as many other great men: it being rarely found that a very fluent elocution, and depth of judgment meet in the same person. His afpect and behaviour ruftic and ungraceful: and this defect was not likely to be rectified in the place where he firft lived, nor afterwards, becaufe the weaknefs of his ftomach would not permit him to ufe his exercifes; he was frequently troubled with the head-ach, and spitting of blood; fpare of diet, and hardly drank any wine. Bafhful to a fault, and when-people crowded to fee him, he would flip into the next fhop, or bye paffage, to avoid them. As this character could not recommend him to the fair fex, he feems to have as little confideration for them as Euripides himfelf. There is hardly the character of one good woman to be found in his poems: he ufes the word [Mulier] but once in the whole Æneis, then too by way of contempt, rendering literally a piece of a verfe out of Homer. In his Paftorals he is full of invectives againft love: in the Georgica he appropriates all the rage of it to the females. He makes Dido, who never deserved that character, lustful and revengeful to the utmost degree; so as to die devoting her lover to destruction; so changeable, that the Destinies themselves could not fix the time of her death; but Iris, the emblem of inconstancy, must determine it. Her sister is something worse. He is so far from passing such a compliment upon Helen, as the grave old counsellor in Homer does, after nine years war, when, upon the sight of her he breaks out into this rapture in the presence of king Priam;

None can the cause of these long wars despise;
The cost bears no proportion to the prize:
Majestic charms in every feature shine;
Her air, her port, her accent is divine.
However, let the fatal beauty go, &c.

Virgil is so far from this complaisant humour, that his heroe falls into an unmanly and ill-timed deliberation, whether he should not kill her in a church; which directly contradicts what Deiphobus says of her, Æneid. VI. in that place where every body tells the truth. He transfers the dogged silence of Ajax's ghost, to that of Dido; though that be no very natural character to an injured lover, or a woman. He brings in the Trojan matrons setting their own fleet on fire; and running afterwards, like witches on their Sabbat, into the woods. He bestows indeed some ornaments on the character of Camilla; but soon abates his favour, by calling her "aspera et horrenda virgo:" He places her in the front of the line for an ill omen of the battle, as one of the ancients has observed. We may observe, on this occasion, it is an art peculiar to Virgil, to intimate the event by some preceding accident. He hardly ever describes the rising of the sun, but with some circumstance which fore-signifies the fortune of the day. For instance, when Æneas leaves Africa and queen Dido, he thus describes the fatal morning.

Tithori croceum linquens aurora cubile.

[And for the remark, we stand indebted to the curious pencil of Pollio] the Mourning fields (Æneid. VI.) are crowded with ladies of a lost reputation: hardly one man gets admittance, and that is Cæneus, for a very good reason. Latinus's queen is turbulent, and ungovernable, and at last hangs herself: and the fair Lavinia is disobedient to the oracle, and to the king, and looks a little flickering after Turnus. I wonder at this the more, because Livy represents her as an excellent person, and who behaved herself with great wisdom in her regency during the minority of her son: so that the poet has done her wrong, and it reflects on her posterity. His goddesses make as ill a figure; Juno is always in a rage, and the fury of heaven: Venus grows so unreasonably confident, as to ask her husband to forge arms for her bastard son; which were enough to provoke one of a more phlegmatic temper than Vulcan was. Notwithstanding all this raillery of Virgil's he was certainly of a very amorous disposition, and has described all that is most delicate in the passion of love; but he conquered his natural inclinations by the help of philosophy; and refined it into friendship, to which he was extremely sensible. The reader will admit of or reject the following conjecture, with the free leave of the writer, who will be equally pleased either way. Virgil had too great an opinion of the influence of the heavenly bodies: and, as an ancient writer says, he was born under the sign of Virgo, with which nativity he much pleased himself, and would exemplify her virtues in his life. Perhaps it was thence that he took his name of Virgil and Parthenias, which does not necessarily signify baseborn. Donatus, and Servius, very good grammarians, give a quite contrary sense of it. He seems to make allusion to this original of his name in that passage,

Illo Virgilium me tempore dulcis alebat
Parthenope.

And this may serve to illustrate his compliment to Cæsar, in which he invites him into his own constellation,

Where, in the void of heaven, a place is free
Betwixt the Scorpion, and the Maid, for thee.

Thus placing him betwixt Juſtice and Power, and in a neighbour manſion to his own; for Virgil ſuppoſed ſouls to aſcend again to their proper and congenial ſtars. Being therefore of this humour, it is no wonder that he refuſed the embraces of the beautiful Plotia, when his indiſcreet friend almoſt threw her into his arms.

But however he ſtood affected to the ladies, there is a dreadful accuſation brought againſt him for the moſt unnatural of all vices, which, by the malignity of human nature, has found more credit in latter times than it did near his own. This took not its riſe ſo much from the Alexis, in which Paſtoral there is not one immodeſt word; as from a ſort of ill nature that will not let any one be without the imputation of ſome vice; and principally becauſe he was ſo ſtrict a follower of Socrates and Plato. In order therefore to his vindication, I ſhall take the matter a little higher.

VIRGIL.

The Cretans were anciently much addicted to navigation, insomuch that it became a Greek proverb, (though omitted, I think, by the industrious Erasmus,) A Cretan that does not know the sea. Their neighbourhood gave them occasion of frequent commerce with the Phœnicians, that accursed people, who infected the western world with endless superstitions, and gross immoralities. From them it is probable, that the Cretans learned this infamous passion, to which they were so much addicted, that Cicero remarks, in his Book de Rep. that it was a disgrace for a young gentleman to be without lovers. Socrates, who was a great admirer of the Cretan constitutions, set his excellent wit to find out some good cause, and use of this evil inclination, and therefore gives an account, wherefore beauty is to be loved in the following passage; for I will not trouble the reader, weary perhaps already, with a long Greek quotation. " There is " but one eternal, immutable, uniform " beauty; in contemplation of which, our " sovereign happiness does consist: and

" therefore a true lover confiders beauty
" and proportion as so many steps and de-
" grees, by which he may ascend from the
" particular to the general, from all that is
" lovely of feature, or regular in propor-
" tion, or charming in sound, to the ge-
" neral fountain of all perfection. And
" if you are so much transported with the
" sight of beautiful persons, as to wish nei-
" ther to eat or drink, but pass your whole
" life in their conversation; to what ecsta-
" sy would it raise you to behold the ori-
" ginal beauty, not filled up with flesh and
" blood, or varnished with a fading mix-
" ture of colours, and the rest of mortal
" trifles and fooleries, but separate, un-
" mixed, uniform, and divine, &c." Thus
far Socrates, in a strain much beyond the
Socraté Cretien of Mr. Balsac: and thus
that admirable man loved his Phædon,
his Charmedes, and Theætetus; and thus
Virgil loved his Alexander, and Cebes,
under the feigned name of Alexis: He received them illiterate, but returned them
to their masters, the one a good poet, and
the other an excellent grammarian; and

to prevent all possible misinterpretations, he warily inserted into the liveliest Episode in the whole Æneis, these words,

Nisus amore pio pueri.

And in the sixth, Quique pii vates. He seems fond of the words, castus, pius, virgo, and the compounds of it; and sometimes stretches the use of that word further than one would think he reasonably should have done, as when he attributes it to Pasiphae herself.

Another vice he is taxed with, is avarice; because he died rich, and so indeed he did in comparison of modern wealth; his estate amounts to near seventy-five thousand pounds of our money: but Donatus does not take notice of this as a thing extraordinary; nor was it esteemed so great a matter, when the cash of a great part of the world lay at Rome. Antony himself bestowed at once two thousand acres of land in one of the best provinces of Italy, upon a ridiculous scribler, who is named by Cicero and Virgil. A late cardinal used to purchase ill flattery at the expence of 100,000 crowns a year. But besides Virgil's other benefactors, he was much in favour with Augustus, whose bounty to him had no limits, but such as the modesty of Virgil prescribed to it. Before he had made his own fortune, he settled his estate upon his own parents and brothers; sent them yearly large sums, so that they lived in great plenty and respect; and at his death divided his estate betwixt duty and gratitude, leaving one half to his relations, and the other to Mecænas, to Tucca and Varius, and a considerable legacy to Augustus, who had introduced a politic fashion of being in every body's will; which alone was a fair revenue for a prince. Virgil shews his detestation of this vice, by placing in the front of the damned those who did not relieve their relations and friends; for the Romans hardly ever extended their liberality further; and therefore I do not remember to have met in all the Latin poets, one character so noble as that short one in Homer.

———— Φίλος δ' ἦν ἀνθρώποισι,
Πάντας γὰρ φιλέεσκε ————

On the other hand, he gives a very advanced place in Elyſium to good patriots, &c. obſerving in all his poem, that rule ſo ſacred amongſt the Romans, that there ſhould be no art allowed, which did not tend to the improvement of the people in virtue. And this was the principle too of our excellent Mr. Waller, who uſed to ſay, that he would raze any line out of his poems, which did not imply ſome motive to virtue; but he was unhappy in the choice of the ſubject of his admirable vein in poetry. The counteſs of Carliſle was the Helen of her country. There is nothing in Pagan philoſophy more true, more juſt, and regular than Virgil's Ethics; and it is hardly poſſible to ſit down to the ſerious peruſal of his works, but a man ſhall riſe more diſpoſed to virtue and goodneſs, as well as moſt agreeably entertained. The contrary to which diſpoſition may happen ſometimes upon the reading of Ovid, of Martial, and ſeveral other ſecond-rate poets. But of the craft and tricking part of life, with which Homer abounds, there is nothing to be found in Virgil; and therefore Plato, who gives the former so many good words, perfumes, crowns, but at last complimentally banishes him his commonwealth, would have intreated Virgil to stay with him, (if they had lived in the same age,) and intrusted him with some important charge in his government. Thus was his life as chaste as his style, and those who can critic his poetry, can never find a blemish in his manners; and one would rather wish to have that purity of mind, which the satyrist himself attributes to him; that friendly disposition, and evenness of temper, and patience, which he was master of in so eminent a degree, than to have the honour of being author of the Æneis, or even of the Georgics themselves.

Having therefore so little relish for the usual amusements of the world, he prosecuted his studies without any considerable interruption, during the whole course of his life, which one may reasonably conjecture to have been something longer than fifty-two years; and therefore it is no

VIRGIL.

wonder that he became the most general scholar that Rome ever bred, unless some one should except Varro. Besides the exact knowledge of rural affairs, he understood medicine, to which profession he was designed by his parents. A curious florist, on which subject one would wish he had writ, as he once intended: so profound a naturalist, that he has solved more phænomena of nature upon sound principles, than Aristotle in his Physics. He studied geometry, the most opposite of all sciences to a poetic genius, and beauties of a lively imagination; but this promoted the order of his narrations, his propriety of language, and clearness of expression, for which he was justly called the pillar of the Latin tongue. This geometrical spirit was the cause, that to fill up a verse he would not insert one superfluous word; and therefore deserves that character which a noble and judicious writer has given him, * "That he never says too little, nor too much." Nor could any

* Essay of Poetry by the Marquis of Normanby.

one ever fill up the verses he left imperfect. There is one supplied near the beginning of the first book; Virgil left the verse thus,

───────Hic illius arma,
Hic currus fuit───────

the rest is none of his.

He was so good a geographer, that he has not only left us the finest description of Italy that ever was; but, besides, was one of the few ancients who knew the true system of the earth, its being inhabited round about, under the torrid zone, and near the poles. Metrodorus, in his five Books of the Zones, justifies him from some exceptions made against him by astronomers. His rhetoric was in such general esteem, that lectures were read upon it in the reign of Tiberius, and the subject of declamations taken out of him. Pollio himself, and many other ancients, commented him. His esteem degenerated into a kind of superstition. The known story of Mr. Cowley is an instance of it.

But the Sortes Virgilianæ were condemned by St. Austin, and other casuists. Abienus, by an odd design, put all Virgil and Livy into Iambic verse; and the pictures of those two were hung in the most honourable place of public libraries; and the design of taking them down, and destroying Virgil's works, was looked upon as one of the most extravagant amongst the many brutish frenzies of Caligula.

PREFACE
TO THE
PASTORALS,

WITH A

Short DEFENCE of VIRGIL againſt ſome of the Reflections of Monſieur FONTENELLE.

Written by WILLIAM WALSH, Eſq.

AS the writings of greateſt antiquity are in verſe, ſo of all ſorts of poetry, Paſtorals ſeem the moſt ancient; being formed upon the model of the firſt innocence, and ſimplicity, which the moderns, better to diſpenſe themſelves from imitating, have wiſely thought fit to treat as fabulous, and impracticable; and yet they, by obeying the unsophisticated dictates of nature, enjoyed the most valuable blessings of life; a vigorous health of body, with a constant serenity and freedom of mind; whilst we, with all our fanciful refinements, can scarcely pass an autumn without some access of a fever, or a whole day, not ruffled by some unquiet passion. He was not then looked upon as a very old man, who reached to a greater number of years, than in these times an ancient family can reasonably pretend to; and we know the names of several, who saw, and practised the world for a longer space of time, than we can read the accounts of in any one entire body of history. In short, they invented the most useful Arts, Pasturage, Tillage, Geometry, Writing, Music, Astronomy, &c. Whilst the moderns, like extravagant heirs, made rich by their industry, ingratefully deride the good old gentleman who left them the estate. It is not therefore to be wondered at, that Pastorals are fallen into disesteem, together with that fashion of life, upon which they were grounded. And, methinks, I see the reader already uneasy at this part of Virgil, counting the pages, and posting to the Æneis; so delightful an entertainment is the very relation of public mischief and slaughter now become to mankind: and yet Virgil passed a much different judgment on his own works; he valued most this part, and his Georgics, and depended upon them for his reputation with posterity: but censures himself, in one of his letters to Augustus, for meddling with heroics, the invention of a degenerating age. This is the reason that the rules of Pastoral are so little known, or studied. Aristotle, Horace, and the Essay of Poetry, take no notice of it. And Mr. Boileau, one of the most accurate of the moderns, because he never loses the ancients out of his sight, bestows scarce half a page on it.

It is the design therefore of the few following pages, to clear this sort of writing from vulgar prejudices; to vindicate our author from some unjust imputations; to look into some of the rules of this sort of poetry, and enquire what sort of versification is most proper for it, in which point we are so much inferior to the ancients, that this consideration alone were enough to make some writers think as they ought, that is, meanly of their own performances.

As all sorts of poetry consist in imitation; Pastoral is the imitation of a shepherd considered under that character: it is requisite therefore to be a little informed of the condition and qualification of these shepherds.

One of the ancients has observed truly, but satyrically enough, that, mankind is the measure of every thing: and thus by a gradual improvement of this mistake, we come to make our own age and country the rule and standard of others, and ourselves at last the measure of them all. We figure the ancient country-men like our own, leading a painful life in poverty and contempt, without wit, or courage, or education: but men had quite different notions of these things, for the first four thousand years of the world; health and strength were then in more esteem than the refinements of pleasure; and it was accounted a great deal more honourable to till the ground, or keep a flock of sheep, than to dissolve in wantonness, and effeminating sloth. Hunting has now an idea of quality joined to it, and is become the most important business in the life of a gentleman; anciently it was quite otherways. Mr. Fleury has severely remarked, that this extravagant passion for hunting is a strong proof of our Gothic extraction, and shews an affinity of humour with the savage Americans. The barbarous Franks and other Germans, (having neither corn, nor wine of their own growth,) when they passed the Rhine, and possessed themselves of countries better cultivated, left the tillage of the land to the old proprietors; and afterwards continued to hazard their lives as freely for their diversion, as they had done before for their necessary subsistence. The English gave this usage the sacred stamp of fashion, and from hence it is that most of our terms of hunting are French. The reader will, I hope, give me his pardon for my freedom on this subject, since an ill accident, occasioned by hunting, kept England in pain, these several months together, for one of the * best, and greatest

* The duke of Shrewsbury.

peers which she has bred for some ages; no less illustrious for civil virtues, and learning, than his ancestors were for all their victories in France.

But there are some prints still left of the ancient esteem for husbandry, and their plain fashion of life, in many of our sir-names, and in the escutcheons of the most ancient families, even those of the greatest kings, the roses, the lilies, the thistle, &c. It is generally known, that one of the principal causes of deposing Mahomet the IVth, was, that he would not allot part of the day to some manual labour, according to the law of Mahomet, and ancient practice of his predecessors. He that reflects on this, will be the less surprised to find that Charlemagne, eight hundred years ago, ordered his children to be instructed in some profession. And eight hundred years yet higher, that Augustus wore no cloaths but such as were made by the hands of the empress and her daughters; and Olympias did the same for Alexander the Great. Nor will he wonder that the Romans, in great exigency, sent for their dictator from the plough, whose whole estate was but of four acres; too little a spot now for the orchard or kitchen garden of a private gentleman. It is commonly known, that the founders of three the most renowned monarchies in the world, were shepherds: and the subject of husbandry has been adorned by the writings and labour of more than twenty kings. It ought not therefore to be matter of surprize to a modern writer, that kings, the shepherds of the people in Homer, laid their first rudiments, in tending their mute subjects; nor that the wealth of Ulysses consisted in flocks and herds, the intendants over which were then in equal esteem with officers of state in latter times. And therefore Eumæus is called Διος ὑφορβος in Homer; not so much because Homer was a lover of a country life, to which he rather seems averse, but by reason of the dignity and greatness of his trust, and because he was the son of a king, stolen away, and sold by the Phœnician pirates; which the ingenious Mr. Cowley seems not to have taken notice of. Nor will it seem strange, that the master of the horse to king Latinus, in the ninth Eneid, was found in the homely employment

of cleaving blocks, when the news of the firſt
ſkirmiſh betwixt the Trojans and Latins was
brought to him.

Being therefore of ſuch quality, they cannot be ſuppoſed ſo very ignorant and unpo-
liſhed; the learning and good breeding of
the world was then in the hands of ſuch
people. He who was choſen by the conſent
of all parties to arbitrate ſo delicate an affair,
as which was the faireſt of the three celebrated beauties of heaven; he who had the ad-
dreſs to debauch away Helen from her huſ-
band, her native country, and from a crown,
underſtood what the French call by the too
ſoft name of Galantérie; he had accompliſh-
ments enough, how ill uſe ſoever he made of
them. It ſeems therefore that Mr. Fontenelle had not duly conſidered the matter,
when he reflected ſo ſeverely upon Virgil, as
if he had not obſerved the laws of decency in
his Paſtorals, in making ſhepherds ſpeak to
things beſide their character, and above their
capacity. " He ſtands amazed that ſhep-
" herds ſhould thunder out, (as he expreſſes
" himſelf,) the formation of the world, and
" that too according to the ſyſtem of Epicu-

"rus." "In truth, (says he, page 176,) I
"cannot tell what to make of this whole
"piece: (the sixth Past.) I can neither com-
"prehend the design of the author, nor the
"connexion of the parts; first come the
"ideas of philosophy, and presently after
"those incoherent fables, &c." To expose
him yet more, he subjoins, "It is Silenus
"himself who makes all this absurd discourse.
"Virgil says, indeed, that he had drank too
"much the day before; perhaps the de-
"bauch hung in his head when he composed
"this poem, &c." Thus far Mr. Fontenelle, who, to the disgrace of reason, as himself ingenuously owns, first built his house,
and then studied architecture; I mean, first
composed his Eclogues, and then studied the
rules. In answer to this, we may observe,
first, that this very Pastoral which he singles
out to triumph over, was recited by a famous
player on the Roman theatre, with marvellous
applause, insomuch that Cicero who had heard
part of it only, ordered the whole to be re-
hearsed; and, struck with admiration of it,
conferred then upon Virgil the glorious title
of

Magnæ spes altera Romæ.

Nor is it old Donatus only who relates this, we have the same account from another very credible and ancient author; so that here we have the judgment of Cicero, and the people of Rome, to confront the single opinion of this adventurous critic. A man ought to be well assured of his own abilities, before he attacks an author of established reputation. If Mr. Fontenelle had perused the fragments of the Phœnician antiquity, traced the progress of learning through the ancient Greek writers, or so much as consulted his learned countryman Huetius, he would have found (which falls out unluckily for him) that a Chaldæan shepherd discovered to the Ægyptians and Greeks the creation of the world. And what subject more fit for such a Pastoral, than that great affair which was first notified to the world by one of that profession? Nor does it appear, (what he takes for granted) that Virgil describes the original of the world according to the hypothesis of Epicurus; he was too well seen in antiquity to commit such a gross mistake; there is not the least men-

THE PASTORALS. 89

tion of chance in that whole passage, nor of the Clinamen Principiorum, so peculiar to Epicurus's hypothesis. Virgil had not only more piety, but was of too nice a judgment to introduce a God denying the power and providence of the Deity, and singing a hymn to the atoms and blind chance. On the contrary, his description agrees very well with that of Moses; and the eloquent commentator D'Acier, who is confident that Horace had perused the sacred history, might with greater reason have affirmed the same thing of Virgil. For, besides the famous passage in the sixth Æneid, (by which this may be illustrated) where the word Principio is used in front of both by Moses and Virgil, and the seas are first mentioned, and the "spiritus intus alit," which might not improbably, as Mr. D'Acier would suggest, allude to the spirit moving upon the face of the waters; but omitting this parallel place, the successive formation of the world is evidently described in these words,

Rerum paulatim sumere formas:

And it is hardly possible to render more literally that verse of Moses,

" Let the waters be gathered into one
" place, and let the dry land appear," than
in this of Virgil,

Jam durare folum, et difcludere Nerea Ponto.

After this the formation of the fun is described (exactly in the Mofaical order,) and next the production of the firſt living creatures, and that too in a fmall number, (ſtill in the fame method,)

Rara per ignotos errent animalia montes.

And here the aforefaid author would probably remark, that Virgil keeps more exactly the Mofaic fyftem, than an ingenious writer, who will by no means allow mountains to be coæval with the world. Thus much will make it probable at leaſt, that Virgil had Mofes in his thoughts rather than Epicurus, when he compofed this poem. But it is further remarkable, that this paſſage was taken from a fong attributed to Apollo, who himfelf too unluckily had been a ſhepherd, and he took it from another yet more ancient, compofed by the firſt inventor of mufic, and

… at that time a shepherd too; and this is one of the noblest fragments of Greek antiquity: and because I cannot suppose the ingenious Mr. Fontenelle one of their number, who pretend to censure the Greeks, without being able to distinguish Greek from Ephesian characters, I shall here set down the lines from which Virgil took this passage, though none of the commentators have observed it.

———————ἐρατὴ δ' οἱ ἔσπετο φωνὴ,
Κραίνων ἀθανάτους τε Θεὸς, καὶ γαῖαν ἐρέμνην,
Ὡς τὰ πρῶτα γένοντο, καὶ ὡς λάχε μοῖραν ἕκαστος, &c.

Thus Linus too began his poem, as appears by a fragment of it preserved by Diogenes Laertius; and the like may be instanced in Musæus himself.

So that our poet here with great judgment, as always, follows the ancient custom of beginning their more solemn songs with the creation, and does it too most properly under the person of a shepherd; and thus the first and best employment of poetry was, to compose hymns in honour of the great Creator of the universe.

Few words will suffice to answer his other

objections. He demands why those several transformations are mentioned in that poem? And is not fable then the life and soul of poetry? Can himself assign a more proper subject of Pastoral, than the Saturnia Regna, the age and scene of this kind of poetry? What theme more fit for the song of a God, or to imprint religious awe, than the omnipotent power of transforming the species of creatures at their pleasure: their families lived in groves, near the clear springs; and what better warning could be given to the hopeful young shepherds, than that they should not gaze too much into the liquid dangerous looking-glass, for fear of being stolen by the water-nymphs, that is, falling and being drowned, as Hylas was? Pasiphae's monstrous passion for a bull is certainly a subject enough fitted for Bucolics. Can Mr. Fontenelle tax Silenus for fetching too far the transformation of the sisters of Phaeton into trees, when perhaps they sat at that very time under the hospitable shade of those alders and poplars? Or the metamorphosis of Philomela into that ravishing bird, which makes the sweetest music of the groves? If he had looked into the ancient Greek writers, or so much as consulted honest Servius, he would have discovered that under the allegory of this drunkenness of Silenus, the refinement and exaltation of mens minds by philosophy was intended. But if the author of these reflexions can take such flights in his wine, it is almost pity that drunkenness should be a sin, or that he should ever want good store of burgundy and champaign. But indeed he seems not to have ever drank out of Silenus's tankard, when he composed either his Critique or Pastorals.

His censure on the fourth seems worse grounded than the other; it is entitled in some ancient manuscripts, The History of the Renovation of the World; he complains " That he cannot understand what is meant " by those many figurative expressions:" but if he had consulted the younger Vossius's dissertation on this Pastoral, or read the excellent oration of the emperor Constantine, made French by a good pen of their own, he would have found there the plain interpretation of all those figurative expressions; and withal, very strong proofs of the truths of the Christian religion; such as converted heathens, as Valerianus, and others: and upon account of this piece, the most learned of all the Latin fathers calls Virgil a Christian, even before Christianity. Cicero takes notice of it in his books of divination, and Virgil probably had put it in verse a considerable time before the edition of his Pastorals. Nor does he appropriate it to Pollio, or his son, but complementally dates it from his consulship. And therefore some one who had not so kind thoughts of Mr. Fontenelle as I, would be inclined to think him as bad a catholic as critic in this place.

But, in respect to some books, he has wrote since, I pass by a great part of this, and shall only touch briefly some of the rules of this sort of poem.

The first is, that an air of piety upon all occasions should be maintained in the whole poem: this appears in all the ancient Greek writers; as Homer, Hesiod, Aratus, &c. And Virgil is so exact in the observation of it, not only in this work, but in his Æneis too, that a celebrated French writer taxes him for permitting Æneas to do nothing without the assistance of some God. But by this it appears at least, that Mr. St. Evremond is no Jansenist.

Mr. Fontenelle seems a little defective in this point; he brings in a pair of shepherdesses disputing very warmly, whether Victoria be a goddess, or a woman. Her great condescension and compassion, her affability and goodness, none of the meanest attributes of the Divinity, pass for convincing arguments that she could not possibly be a goddess.

> Les déesses toûjours fieres et méprisantes
>   Ne rassureroient point les bergeres trem-
>   blantes
>   Par d'obligeans discours, des souris gracieux;
>   Mais tu l'as veu; cette auguste personne
>   Qui vient de paroistre en ces lieux
>   Prend soin de rassurer au moment qu'elle
>   etonne,
>   Sa bonté descendant sans peine jusqu'à nous.

In short, she has too many divine perfections to be a Deity, and therefore she is a mortal [which was the thing to be proved.] It is directly contrary to the practice of all ancient poets, as well as to the rules of decency and religion, to make such odious preferences. I am much surprised therefore that he should use such an argument as this:

> Cloris, as tu veu des déesses
> Avoir un air si facile et si doux?

Was not Aurora, and Venus, and Luna, and I know not how many more of the heathen deities, too easy of access to Tithonus, to Anchises, and to Endymion? Is there any thing more sparkish and better-humoured than Venus' accosting her son in the desarts of Libya? or than the behaviour of Pallas to Diomedes, one of the most perfect and admirable pieces of all the Iliads; where she condescends to raillé him so agreeably; and notwithstanding her severe virtue, and all the ensigns of majesty, with which she so terribly adorns herself, condescends to ride with him in his chariot? But the Odysses are full of greater instances of condescension than this.

This brings to mind that famous passage of Lucan, in which he prefers Cato to all the Gods at once.

Victrix causa diis placuit, sed victa Catoni.

Which Bræleuf has rendered so flatly, and which may be thus paraphrased;

Heaven meanly with the conqueror did comply,
But Cato rather than submit would die.

It is an unpardonable presumption in any sort of religion, to compliment their princes at the expence of their deities.

But letting that pass, this whole Eclogue is but a long paraphrase of a trite verse in Virgil, and Homer.

Nec vox hominem sonat, O Dea certe.

So true is that remark of the admirable earl of Roscommon, if applied to the Romans, rather I fear than to the English, since his own death.

———— one sterling line,
Drawn to French wire, would thro' whole
  pages shine.

Another rule is, that the characters should represent that ancient innocence, and unpractised plainness, which was then in the world. P. Rapin has gathered many instances of this out of Theocritus, and Virgil; and the reader can do it as well as himself. But Mr. Fontenelle transgressed this rule, when he hid himself in the thicket to listen to the private discourse of the two shepherdesses. This is not only ill breeding at Versailles; the Arcadian shepherdesses themselves would have set their dogs upon one for such an unpardonable piece of rudeness.

A third rule is, that there should be some ordonnance, some design, or little plot, which may deserve the title of a pastoral scene. This is every where observed by Virgil, and particularly remarkable in the first Eclogue; the standard of all pastorals; a beautiful landscape presents itself to your view, a shepherd with his flock around him, resting securely under a spreading beach, which furnished the first food to our ancestors. Another in a quite different situation of mind and circumstances, the sun setting, the hospitality of the more fortunate shepherd, &c. And here Mr. Fontenelle seems not a little wanting.

A fourth rule, and of great importance in this delicate sort of writing, is, that there be choice diversity of subjects; that the Eclogue, like a beautiful prospect, should charm by its variety. Virgil is admirable in this point, and far surpasses Theocritus, as he does every where, when judgment and contrivance have the principal part. The subject of the First Pastoral is hinted above.

The Second contains the love of Coridon for Alexis, and the seasonable reproach he gives himself, that he left his vines half pruned, (which according to the Roman rituals, derived a curse upon the fruit that grew upon it) whilst he pursued an object undeserving his passion.

The Third, a sharp contention of two shepherds for the prize of poetry.

The Fourth contains the discourse of a shepherd comforting himself in a declining age, that a better was ensuing.

The Fifth a lamentation for a dead friend, the firſt draught of which is probably more ancient than any of the Paſtorals now extant; his brother being at firſt intended; but he afterwards makes his court to Auguſtus, by turning it into an apotheoſis of Julius Cæſar.

The Sixth is the Silenus.

The Seventh, another poetical diſpute, firſt compoſed at Mantua.

The Eighth is the deſcription of a deſpairing lover, and a magical charm.

He ſets the Ninth after all theſe, very modeſtly, becauſe it was particular to himſelf; and here he would have ended that work, if Gallus had not prevailed upon him to add one more in his favour.

Thus curious was Virgil in diverſifying his ſubjects. But Mr. Fontenelle is a great deal too uniform; begin where you pleaſe, the ſubject is ſtill the ſame. We find it true what he ſays of himſelf.

Toûjours, toûjours de l'amour.

He ſeems to take paſtorals and love-verſes for the ſame thing. Has human nature no

THE PASTORALS. 101

other paſſion? does not fear, ambition, avarice, pride, a capricio of honour, and lazineſs itſelf often triumph over love? But this paſſion does all, not only in paſtorals, but in modern tragedies too. A hero can no more fight, or be ſick, or die, than he can be born, without a woman. But dramatics have been compoſed in compliance to the humour of the age, and the prevailing inclination of the great, whoſe example has a more powerful influence, not only in the little court behind the ſcenes, but on the great theatre of the world. However, this inundation of love-verſes is not ſo much an effect of their amorouſneſs, as of immoderate ſelf-love. This being the only ſort of poetry, in which the writer can, not only without cenſure, but even with commendation, talk of himſelf. There is generally more of the paſſion of Narciſſus, than concern for Chloris and Corinna, in this whole affair. Be pleaſed to look into almoſt any of thoſe writers, and you ſhall meet every where that eternal 'moy,' which the admirable Paſchal ſo judiciouſly condemns. Homer can never be enough admired for this one ſo particular quality, that he never speaks of himself, either in the Iliad, or the Odysseys; and if Horace had never told us his genealogy, but left it to the writer of his life, perhaps he had not been a loser by it. This consideration might induce those great critics, Varius and Tucca, to raze out the four first verses of the Æneis, in great measure, for the sake of that unlucky "ille ego." But extraordinary geniuses have a sort of prerogative, which may dispense them from laws, binding to subject wits. However, the ladies have the less reason to be pleased with those addresses, of which the poet takes the greater share to himself. Thus the beau presses into their dressing-room, but it is not so much to adore their fair eyes, as to adjust his own steenkirk and peruke, and set his countenance in their glass.

A fifth rule, (which one may hope will not be contested) is, that the writer should shew in his compositions, some competent skill of the subject matter, that which makes the character of persons introduced. In this, as in all other points of learning, decency, and œconomy of a poem, Virgil much excels his master Theocritus. The poet is better skilled in husbandry than those that get their bread by it. He describes the nature, the diseases, the remedies, the proper places, and seasons, of feeding, of watering their flocks; the furniture, diet; the lodging and pastimes of his shepherds. But the persons brought in by Mr. Fontenelle are shepherds in masquerade, and handle their sheep-hook as aukwardly, as they do their oaten reed. They saunter about with their " chers moutons," but they relate as little to the business in hand, as the painter's dog, or a Dutch ship, does to the history designed. One would suspect some of them, that instead of leading out their sheep into the plains of Mount-Briton, and Marcilli, to the flowry banks of Lignon, or the Charanthe; that they are driving directly à la Boucherie, to make money of them. I hope hereafter Mr. Fontenelle will choose his servants better.

A sixth rule is, that as the style ought to be natural, clear, and elegant, it should have some peculiar relish of the ancient fashion of writing. Parables in these times were frequently used, as they are still by the eastern nations, philosophical questions, ænigma's, &c. and of this we find instances in the sacred writings, in Homer, contemporary with king David, in Herodotus, in the Greek tragedians; this piece of antiquity is imitated by Virgil with great judgment and discretion: he has proposed one riddle, which has never yet been solved by any of his commentators. Though he knew the rules of rhetoric, as well as Cicero himself, he conceals that skill in his Pastorals, and keeps close to the character of antiquity: nor ought the connexions and transitions to be very strict and regular; this would give the Pastorals an air of novelty; and of this neglect of exact connexions, we have instances in the writings of the ancient Chineses, of the Jews and Greeks, in Pindar, and other writers of dithyrambics, in the choruses of Æschylus, Sophocles, and Euripides. If Mr. Fontenelle and Ruæus had considered this, the one would have spared his critique of the sixth, and the other, his reflexions upon the ninth Pastoral. The overscrupulous care of connexions, makes the modern compositions oftentimes tedious and flat: and by the omission of them it comes to pass, that the Pensées of the incomparable Mr. Paschal, and perhaps of Mr. Bruyere, are two of the most entertaining books which the modern French can boast of. Virgil, in this point, was not only faithful to the character of antiquity, but copies after nature herself. Thus a meadow, where the beauties of the spring are profusely blended together, makes a more delightful prospect, than a curious parterre of sorted flowers in our gardens, and we are much more transported with the beauty of the heavens, and admiration of their Creator, in a clear night, when we behold stars of all magnitudes, promiscuously moving together, than if those glorious lights were ranked in their several orders, or reduced into the finest geometrical figures.

Another rule omitted by P. Rapin, as some of his are by me, (for I do not design an intire treatise in this preface) is, that not only the sentences should be short and smart, upon which account he justly blames the Italian, and French, as too talkative, but that the whole piece should be so too. Virgil transgressed this rule in his first Pastorals, I mean those which he composed at Mantua, but rectified the fault in his riper years. This appears by the Culex, which is as long as five of his Pastorals put together. The greater part of those he finished, have less than an hundred verses, and but two of them exceed that number. But the Silenus, which he seems to have designed for his master-piece, in which he introduces a god singing, and he too full of inspiration, which is intended by that ebriety, (which Mr. Fontenelle so unreasonably ridicules,) though it go through so vast a field of matter, and comprises the mythology of near two thousand years, consists but of fifty lines; so that its brevity is no less admirable, than the subject matter; the noble fashion of handling it, and the Deity speaking. Virgil keeps up his characters in this respect too, with the strictest decency. For poetry and pastime was not the business of men's lives in those days, but only their seasonable recreation after necessary labours. And therefore the length of some of the modern Italian, and English compositions, is against the rules of this kind of poesy.

THE PASTORALS.

I shall add something very briefly, touching the versification of Pastorals, though it be a mortifying consideration to the moderns. Heroic verse, as it is commonly called, was used by the Greeks in this sort of poem, as very ancient and natural: lyrics, iambics, &c. being invented afterwards: but there is so great a difference in the numbers, of which it may be compounded, that it may pass rather for a genus, than species, of verse. Whosoever shall compare the numbers of the three following verses, will quickly be sensible of the truth of this observation.

Tityre, tu patulæ recubans sub tegmine fagi.

The first of the Georgics,

Quid faciat lætas segetes, quo sydere terram,

and of the Æneis,

Arma, virumque cano, Trojæ qui primus ab oris.

The sound of the verses, is almost as different as the subjects. But the Greek writers of Pastoral, usually limited themselves to the example of the first; which Virgil found so exceeding difficult, that he quitted it, and left the honour of that part to Theocritus. It is indeed probable, that what we improperly call rhyme, is the most ancient sort of poetry; and learned men have given good arguments for it; and therefore a French historian commits a gross mistake, when he attributes that invention to a king of Gaul, as an English gentleman does, when he makes a Roman emperor the inventor of it. But the Greeks, who understood fully the force and power of numbers, soon grew weary of this childish sort of verse, as the younger Vossius justly calls it, and therefore those rhyming hexameters, which Plutarch observes in Homer himself, seem to be the remains of a barbarous age. Virgil had them in such abhorrence, that he would rather make a false syntax, than what we call a rhyme. Such a verse as this,

Vir precor uxori, frater succurre sorori,

was passable in Ovid. but the nicer ears in Augustus's court could not pardon Virgil for

At regina pyra.

So that the principal ornament of modern poetry, was accounted deformity by the Latins and Greeks; it was they who invented the different terminations of words, those happy compositions, those short monosyllables, those transpositions for the elegance of the sound and sense, which are wanting so much in modern languages. The French sometimes crowd together ten or twelve monosyllables, into one disjointed verse; they may understand the nature of, but cannot imitate, those wonderful spondees of Pythagoras, by which he could suddenly pacify a man that was in a violent transport of anger; nor those swift numbers of the priests of Cybele, which had the force to enrage the most sedate and phlegmatic tempers. Nor can any modern put into his own language the energy of that single poem of Catullus.

Super alta vectus Atys, &c.

Latin is but a corrupt dialect of Greek; and the French, Spanish, and Italian a corruption of Latin; and therefore a man might as well go about to persuade me that vinegar is a nobler liquor than wine, as that the modern compositions can be as graceful and harmonious as the Latin itself. The Greek tongue very naturally falls into iambics, and therefore the diligent reader may find six or seven and twenty of them in those accurate orations of Isocrates. The Latin as naturally falls into heroic; and therefore the beginning of Livy's history is half an hexameter, and that of Tacitus an intire one. * The Roman historian describing the glorious effort of a colonel to break through a brigade of the enemies, just after the defeat at Cannæ, falls unknowingly into a verse not unworthy Virgil himself.

> Hæc ubi dicta dedit, stringit gladium, cuneoque
> Facto per medios, &c.

Ours and the French can at best but fall into blank verse, which is a fault in prose. The misfortune indeed is common to us both, but we deserve more compassion, because we are not vain of our barbarities. As age brings men back into the state and infirmities

* Livy.

of childhood, upon the fall of their empire the Romans doted into rhyme, as appears sufficiently by the hymns of the Latin church; and yet a great deal of the French poetry does hardly deserve that poor title. I shall give an instance out of a poem which had the good luck to gain the prize in 1685, for the subject deserved a nobler pen.

> Tous les jours ce grand roy des outres roys
> l'example,
> S'ouvre nouveau chemin au faiste de un ton
> temple, &c.

The judicious Malherbe exploded this sort of verse near eighty years ago. Nor can I forbear wondering at that passage of a famous academician, in which he, most compassionately, excuses the ancients for their not being so exact in their compositions as the modern French, because they wanted a dictionary, of which the French are at last happily provided. If Demosthenes and Cicero had been so lucky as to have had a dictionary, and such a patron as Cardinal Richelieu, perhaps they might have aspired to the honour of Balzac's Legacy of Ten Pounds, " le prix de l'eloquence."

On the contrary, I dare assert that there are hardly ten lines in either of those great orators, or even in the catalogue of Homer's ships, which is not more harmonious, more truly rythmical, than most of the French or English sonnets; and therefore they lose, at least, one half of their native beauty by translation.

I cannot but add one remark on this occasion, that the French verse is oftentimes not so much as rhyme, in the lowest sense; for the childish repetition of the same note cannot be called music; such instances are infinite, as in the forecited poem.

  'Epris Trophée caché;
  Mepris Orphée cherché.

Mr. Boileau himself has a great deal of this μετοτευία, not by his own neglect, but purely by the faultiness and poverty of the French tongue. Mr. Fontenelle at last goes into the excessive paradoxes of Mr. Perrault, and boasts of the vast number of their excellent songs, preferring them to the Greek and

THE PASTORALS.

Latin. But an ancient writer of as good credit has assured us, that seven lives would hardly suffice to read over the Greek odes; but a few weeks would be sufficient, if a man were so very idle, as to read over all the French. In the mean time, I should be very glad to see a catalogue of but fifty of theirs with

* Exact propriety of word and thought.

Notwithstanding all the high encomiums and mutual gratulations which they give one another (for I am far from censuring the whole of that illustrious society, to which the learned world is much obliged) after all those golden dreams at the L'Ouvre, that their pieces will be as much valued ten or twelve ages hence, as the ancient Greek, or Roman, I can no more get it into my head, that they will last so long than I could believe the learned Dr. H―― K. [of the Royal Society,] if he should pretend to shew me a butterfly that had lived a thousand winters.

* Essay of Poetry.

When Mr. Fontenelle wrote his Eclogues, he was so far from equalling Virgil or Theocritus, that he had some pains to take before he could understand in what the principal beauty, and graces of their writings do consist.

To Mr. DRYDEN,

On his Excellent Translation of VIRGIL.

WHENE'ER great Virgil's lofty verse I see,
    The pompous scene charms my admiring
       eye:
There different beauties in perfection meet;
The thoughts as proper, as the numbers sweet:
And when wild fancy mounts a daring height,
Judgment steps in, and moderates her flight.
Wisely he manages his wealthy store,
Still says enough, and yet implies still more:
For tho' the weighty sense be closely wrought,
The reader's left t'improve the pleasing thought.

  Hence we despair to see an English dress
Should e'er his nervous energy express;
For who could that in fetter'd rhyme inclose,
Which without loss can scarce be told in prose!

  But you, great Sir, his manly genius raise;
And make your copy share an equal praise.
Oh how I see thee in soft scenes of love,
Renew those passions he alone could move!

Here Cupid's charms are with new art exprest,
And pale Eliza leaves her peaceful rest:
Leaves her Elysium, as if glad to live,
To love, and wish, to sigh, despair, and grieve,
And die again for him that would again deceive.
Nor does the mighty Trojan less appear
Than Mars himself amidst the storms of war.
Now his fierce eyes with double fury glow,
And a new dread attends th' impending blow:
The Daunian chiefs their eager rage abate,
And, tho' unwounded, seem to feel their fate.

Long the rude fury of an ignorant age,
With barbarous spite, prophan'd his sacred page.
The heavy Dutchmen, with laborious toil,
Wrested his sense, and cramp'd his vigorous style;
No time, no pains the drudging pedants spare;
But still his shoulders must the burden bear.
While thro' the mazes of their comments led,
We learn not what he writes, but what they read.
Yet, thro' these shades of undistinguish'd night
Appear'd some glimmering intervals of light;
Till mangled by a vile translating sect,
Like babes by witches in effigy rackt;

Till Ogleby, mature in dulness, rose,
And Holborn doggrel, and low chiming prose,
His strength and beauty did at once depose.
But now the magic spell is at an end,
Since even the dead in you hath found a friend;
You free the bard from rude oppressors' power,
And grace his verse with charms unknown before:
He, doubly thus oblig'd, must doubting stand,
Which chiefly should his gratitude command;
Whether should claim the tribute of his heart,
The patron's bounty, or the poet's art.

Alike with wonder and delight we view'd
The Roman genius in thy verse renew'd:
We saw thee raise soft Ovid's amorous fire,
And fit the tuneful Horace to thy lyre:
We saw new gall imbitter Juv'nal's pen,
And crabbed Perseus made politely plain:
Virgil alone was thought too great a task;
What you could scarce perform, or we durst ask:
A task! which Waller's muse could ne'er engage;
A task! too hard for Denham's stronger rage:
Sure of success they some flight sallies try'd,
But the fenc'd coast their bold attempts defy'd.

With fear their o'er-match'd forces back they drew,
Quitted the province Fate reserv'd for you.
In vain thus Philip did the Persians storm;
A work his son was destin'd to perform.

" O had Roscommon * liv'd to hail the day,
" And sing loud Pæans thro' the crowded way,
" When you in Roman majesty appear,
" Which none know better, and none come so
    " near:"
The happy author wou'd with wonder see,
His rules were only prophecies of thee:
And were he now to give translators light,
He'd bid them only read thy work, and write.

For this great task our loud applause is due;
We own old favours, but must press for new:
Th' expecting world demands one labour more;
And thy lov'd Homer does thy aid implore,
To right his injur'd works, and set them free
From the lewd rhymes of groveling Ogleby.
Then shall his verse in grateful pomp appear,
Nor will his birth renew the ancient jar;
On those Greek cities we shall look with scorn,
And in our Britain think the poet born.

  * Essay of Translated Verse, page 26.

To Mr. DRYDEN,

On his Translation of VIRGIL.

I.

WE read, how dreams and visions heretofore
. The prophet and the poet cou'd inspire;
And make 'em in unusual rapture soar,
With rage divine, and with poetic fire.

II.

O could I find it now;—Wou'd Virgil's shade
But for a while vouchsafe to bear the light;
To grace my numbers, and that muse to aid,
Who sings the poet that has done him right.

III.

It long has been this sacred author's fate,
To lie at every dull translator's will;
Long, long his muse has groan'd beneath the weight
Of mangling Ogleby's presumptuous quill.

IV.

Dryden, at last, in his defence arose;
The father now is righted by the son:
And while his Muse endeavours to disclose
That poet's beauties, she declares her own.

V.

In your smooth, pompous numbers drest, each line,
Each thought, betrays such a majestic touch;
He cou'd not, had he finish'd his design,
Have wish'd it better, or have done so much.

VI.

You, like his hero, though yourself were free:
And disentangl'd from the war of wit;
You, who secure might other dangers see,
And safe from all malicious censures sit.

VII.

Yet because sacred Virgil's noble muse,
O'erlay'd by fools, was ready to expire:
To risk your fame again, you boldly chuse,
Or to redeem, or perish with your fire.

VIII.

Ev'n first and last, we owe him half to you,
For that his Æneids miss'd their threatned fate,
Was—that his friends by some prediction knew,
Hereafter, who correcting should translate.

IX.

But hold, my muse, thy needless flight restrain,
Unless like him thou coud'st a verse indite:
   To think his fancy to describe, is vain,
   Since nothing can discover light, but light.

X.

   'Tis want of genius that does more deny:
   'Tis fear my praise shou'd make your glory less.
   And therefore, like the modest painter, I,
   Must draw the veil, where I cannot express.

HENRY GRAHME.

To Mr. DRYDEN.

NO undisputed monarch govern'd yet
    With universal sway the realms of wit;
Nature cou'd never such expence afford;
Each several province own'd a several lord.
A poet then had his poetic wife,
One Muse embrac'd, and married for his life.
By the stale thing his appetite was cloy'd,
His fancy lessen'd, and his fire destroy'd.
But nature grown extravagantly kind,
With all her treasures did adorn your mind.

The different powers were then united found,
And you wit's universal monarch crown'd:
Your mighty sway your great desert secures,
And ev'ry Muse and ev'ry Grace is yours,
To none confin'd, by turns you all enjoy,
Sated with this, you to another fly.
So Sultan-like in your seraglio stand,
While wishing Muses wait for your command.
Thus no decay, no want of vigour find,
Sublime your fancy, boundless is your mind.
Not all the blasts of time can do you wrong;
Young, spite of age; in spite of weakness, strong.
Time, like Alcides, strikes you to the ground:
You, like Antæus, from each fall rebound.

H. St. John.

To Mr. DRYDEN, on his VIRGIL.

'TIS said that Phidias gave such living grace
   To the carv'd image of a beauteous face,
That the cold marble might even seem to be
The life; and the true life, the imag'ry.

You pass'd that artist, Sir, and all his powers,
Making the best of Roman poets yours;
With such effect, we know not which to call
The imitation, which th' original.

What Virgil lent, you pay in equal weight,
  The charming beauty of the coin no less;
  And such the majesty of your impress,
You seem the very author you translate.

'Tis certain, were he now alive with us,
  And did revolving destiny constrain,
  To dress his thoughts in English o'er again,
Himself cou'd write no otherwise than thus.

His old encomium never did appear
  So true as now; Romans and Greeks submit,
  Something of late is in our language writ,
More nobly great than the fam'd Iliads were.

JA. WRIGHT.

To Mr. DRYDEN,

On his TRANSLATIONS.

AS flow'rs transplanted from a southern sky,
But hardly bear, or in the raising die,
Missing their native sun, at best retain
But a faint odour, and but live with pain:
So Roman poetry by moderns taught,
Wanting the warmth with which his author wrote,
Is a dead image, and a worthless draught.
While we transfuse, the nimble spirit flies,
Escapes unseen, evaporates, and dies.

Who then attempts to shew the antients wit,
Must copy with the genius that they writ.
Whence we conclude from thy translated song,
So just, so warm, so smooth, and yet so strong,
Thou, heav'nly charmer! soul of harmony!
That all their geniuses reviv'd in thee.

Thy trumpet sounds, the dead are rais'd to light,
New-born they rise, and take to heav'n their flight;

Deckt in thy verse, as clad with rays, they shine
All glorify'd, immortal, and divine.

As Britain, in rich soil abounding wide,
Furnish'd for use, for luxury, and pride,
Yet spreads her wanton sails on ev'ry shore,
For foreign wealth, insatiate still of more;
To her own wool, the silks of Asia joins,
And to her plenteous harvests, Indian mines:
So Dryden, not contented with the fame
Of his own works, tho' an immortal name,
To lands remote he sends his learned muse,
The noblest seeds of foreign wit to chuse,
Feasting our sense so many various ways,
Say is't thy bounty, or thy thirst of praise?
That by comparing others, all might see,
Who most excell'd, are yet excell'd by thee.

GEORGE GRANVILLE.

VIRGIL's
PASTORALS.

PASTORAL I.

THE ARGUMENT.

The occasion of the first Pastoral was this: When Augustus had settled himself in the Roman empire, that he might reward his veteran troops for their past service, he distributed among them all the lands that lay about Cremona and Mantua: turning out the right owners for having sided with his enemies. Virgil was a sufferer among the rest; who afterwards recovered his estate by Mæcænas's intercession, and as an instance of his gratitude composed the following Pastoral; where he sets out his own good fortune in the person of Tityrus, and the calamities of his Mantuan neighbours in the character of Melibæus.

THE
FIRST PASTORAL:
OR,
TITYRUS AND MELIBŒUS.

MELIBŒUS.

BENEATH the shade which beechen
    boughs diffuse,
You, Tityrus, entertain your sylvan muse:
Round the wide world in banishment we roam,
Forc'd from our pleasing fields and native home:
While stretched at ease you sing your happy loves; 5.
And Amarillis fills the shady groves.

TITYRUS.

These blessings, friend, a Deity bestow'd:
For never can I deem him less than God.

The tender firstlings of my woolly breed
Shall on his holy altar often bleed.   10
He gave my kine to graze the flow'ry plain;
And to my pipe renew'd the rural strain.

MELIBŒUS.

I envy not your fortune, but admire,
That while the raging sword and wasteful fire
Destroy the wretched neighbourhood around,   15
No hostile arms approach your happy ground.
Far diff'rent is my fate: my feeble goats
With pains I drive from their forsaken cotes:
And this you see I scarcely drag along,
Who yeaning on the rocks has left her young;   20
(The hope and promise of my failing fold.)
My loss by dire portents the gods foretold:
For had I not been blind, I might have seen
Yon riven oak, the fairest of the green,
And the hoarse raven, on the blasted bough.   25
By croaking from the left presag'd the coming blow.
But tell me, Tityrus, what heav'nly power
Preserv'd your fortunes in that fatal hour!

TITYRUS.

Fool that I was, I thought imperial Rome
Like Mantua, where on market-days we come, 30
And thither drive our tender lambs from home.
So kids and whelps their fires and dams express:
And so the great I measur'd by the less.
But country towns, compar'd with her, appear
Like shrubs, when lofty cypresses are near. 35

MELIBŒUS.

What great occasion call'd you hence to Rome?

TITYRUS.

Freedom, which came at length, tho' slow to
    come:
Nor did my search of liberty begin,
Till my black hairs were chang'd upon my chin.
Nor Amarillis would vouchsafe a look, 40
Till Galatea's meaner bonds I broke.
Till then a helpless, hopeless, homely swain,
I sought not freedom, nor aspir'd to gain:
Tho' many a victim from my folds was bought,
And many a cheese to country markets brought, 45

Yet all the little that I got, I spent,
And still return'd as empty as I went.

MELIBŒUS.

We stood amaz'd to see your mistress mourn;
Unknowing that she pin'd for your return:
We wonder'd why she kept her fruit so long, 50
For whom so late th' ungather'd apples hung;
But now the wonder ceases, since I see
She kept them only, Tityrus, for thee.
For thee the bubbling springs appear'd to mourn,
And whisp'ring pines made vows, for thy return. 55

TITYRUS.

What should I do? while here I was en-
    chain'd,
No glimpse of godlike liberty remain'd;
Nor cou'd I hope in any place but there,
To find a god so present to my pray'r.
There first the youth of heav'nly birth I view'd, 60
For whom our monthly victims are renew'd.
He heard my vows, and graciously decreed
My grounds to be restor'd, my former flocks to
    feed.

MELIBŒUS.

O fortunate old man! whose farm remains
For you sufficient, and requires your pains: 65
Tho' rushes overspread the neighb'ring plains.
Tho' here the marshy grounds approach your fields,
And there the soil a stony harvest yields.
Your teeming ewes shall no strange meadows try,
Nor fear a rott from tainted company. 70
Behold yon bord'ring fence of sallow trees
Is fraught with flow'rs, the flow'rs are fraught
    with bees:
The busy bees with a soft murm'ring strain
Invite to gentle sleep the lab'ring swain.
While from the neighb'ring rock, with rural
    songs 75
The pruner's voice the pleasing dream prolongs;
Stock-doves and turtles tell their am'rous pain,
And, from the lofty elms, of love complain.

TITYRUS.

Th' inhabitants of seas and skies shall change,
And fish on shore, and stags in air shall range, 80
The banish'd Parthian dwell on Arar's brink,
And the blue German shall the Tigris drink,

Ere I, forsaking gratitude and truth,
Forget the figure of that godlike youth.

MELIBŒUS.

But we must beg our bread in climes un-
  known,   85
Beneath the scorching or the freezing zone.
And some to far Oaxis shall be sold;
Or try the Lybian heat, or Scythian cold.
The rest among the Britons be confin'd;
A race of men from all the world disjoin'd. 90
O must the wretched exiles ever mourn,
Nor after length of rolling years return;
Are we condemn'd by fate's unjust decree,
No more our houses and our homes to see?
Or shall we mount again the rural throne, 95
And rule the country kingdome, once our own?
Did we for these barbarians plant and sow,
On these, on these, our happy fields bestow?
Good heav'n, what dire effects from civil discord
  flow!
Now let me graff my pears, and prune the vine; 100
The fruit is theirs, the labour only mine.
Farewel my pastures, my paternal stock;
My fruitful fields, and my more fruitful flock!

No more, my goats, shall I behold you climb
The steepy cliffs, or crop the flow'ry thyme!   105.
No more extended in the grot below,
Shall see you browzing on the mountain's brow
The prickly shrubs; and after on the bare,
Lean down the deep abyss, and hang in air.
No more my sheep shall sip the morning dew;   110
No more my song shall please the rural crew:
Adieu, my tuneful pipe! and all the world adieu!

TITYRUS.

This night, at least, with me forget your care;
Chesnuts and curds and cream shall be your fare:
The carpet-ground shall be with leaves o'er-
    spread;   115
And boughs shall weave a cov'ring for your head.
For see yon sunny hill the shade extends;
And curling smoke from cottages ascends.

VIRGIL's PASTORALS.

PASTORAL II.

THE ARGUMENT.

The commentators can by no means agree on the person of Alexis, but are all of opinion that some beautiful youth is meant, by him, to whom Virgil here makes love, in Corydon's language and simplicity. His way of courtship is wholly pastoral: he complains of the boy's coyness; recommends himself for his beauty and skill in piping; invites the youth into the country, where he promises him the diversions of the place, with a suitable present of nuts and apples: but when he finds nothing will prevail, he resolves to quit his troublesome amour, and betake himself again to his former business.

THE

SECOND PASTORAL.

OR,

ALEXIS.

Young Corydon, th' unhappy shepherd swain,
  The fair Alexis lov'd, but lov'd in vain:
And underneath the beechen shade, alone,
Thus to the woods and mountains made his moan.
Is this, unkind Alexis, my reward,   5
And must I die unpitied and unheard?
Now the green lizard in the grove is laid,
The sheep enjoy the coolness of the shade;
And Thestylis wild thyme and garlick beats
For harvest hinds, o'erspent with toil and heats:
While in the scorching sun I trace in vain   10
Thy flying footsteps o'er the burning plain,

The creaking locusts with my voice conspire,
They fry'd with heat and I with fierce desire.
How much more easy was it to sustain   15
Proud Amarillis and her haughty reign,
The scorns of young Menalcas, once my care,
Tho' he was black, and thou art heav'nly fair.
Trust not too much to that enchanting face;
Beauty's a charm, but soon the charm will pass:
White lilies lie neglected on the plain,   20
While dusky hyacinths for use remain.
My passion is thy scorn: nor wilt thou know
What wealth I have, what gifts I can bestow:
What stores my dairies and my folds contain;   25
A thousand lambs that wander on the plain:
New milk that all the winter never fails,
And all the summer overflows the pails:
Amphion sung not sweeter to his herd,
When summon'd stones the Theban turrets rear'd.
Nor am I so deform'd; for late I stood
Upon the margin of the briny flood:
The winds were still; and if the glass be true,
With Daphnis I may vie, tho' judg'd by you.
O leave the noisy town, O come and see   35
Our country cotts, and live content with me!

To wound the flying deer, and from their cotes
With me to drive a-field the browzing goats;
To pipe and sing, and in our country strain
To copy, or perhaps contend with Pan. 40
Pan taught to join with wax, unequal reeds,
Pan loves the shepherds, and their flocks he feeds,
Nor scorn the pipe; Amyntas, to be taught,
With all his kisses wou'd my skill have bought.
Of seven smooth joints a mellow pipe I have, 45
Which with his dying breath Damætus gave:
And said, this, Corydon, I leave to thee;
For only thou deserv'st it after me.
His eyes Amyntas durst not upward lift,
For much he grudg'd the praise, but more the gift. 50
Besides two kids that in the valley stray'd
I found by chance, and to my fold convey'd;
They drain two bagging udders every day;
And these shall be companions of thy play.
Both fleck'd with white, the true Arcadian strain, 55
Which Thestylis had often begg'd in vain:
And she shall have them, if again she sues,
Since you the giver and the gift refuse.
Come to my longing arms, my lovely care,
And take the presents, which the nymphs prepare. 60

White lilies in full canisters they bring,
With all the glories of the purple spring.
The daughters of the flood have search'd the mead
For violets pale, and crop'd the poppy's head;
The short narcissus and fair daffodil, 65
Pansies to please the sight, and cassia sweet to smell;
And set soft hyacinths with iron-blue,
To shade marsh marigolds of shining hue.
Some bound in order, others loosely strow'd,
To dress thy bow'r, and trim thy new abode. 70
Myself will search our planted grounds at home,
For downy peaches and the glossy plumb:
And thrash the chesnuts in the neighb'ring grove,
Such as my Amarillis us'd to love.
The laurel and the myrtle sweets agree; 75
And both in nosegays shall be bound for thee.
Ah, Corydon, ah poor unhappy swain,
Alexis will thy homely gifts disdain:
Nor shouldst thou offer all thy little store,
Will rich Iolas yield, but offer more. 80
What have I done, to name that wealthy swain,
So powerful are his presents, mine so mean!
The bear amidst my chrystal streams I bring;
And southern winds to blast my flow'ry spring.

Ah cruel creature, whom dost thou despise? 85
The gods to live in woods have left the skies.
And godlike Paris in th' Idean grove,
To Priam's wealth preferr'd Oenone's love.
In cities which she built, let Pallas reign;
Tow'rs are for gods, but forests for the swain. 90
The greedy lioness the wolf pursues,
The wolf the kid, the wanton kid the browse:
Alexis thou art chas'd by Corydon;
All follow sev'ral games, and each his own.
See from afar the fields no longer smoke, 95
The sweating steers unharness'd from the yoke,
Bring, as in triumph, back the crooked plough;
The shadows lengthen as the sun goes low.
Cool breezes now the raging heats remove;
Ah, cruel heav'n! that made no cure for love! 100
I wish for balmy sleep, but wish in vain:
Love has no bounds in pleasure, or in pain.
What frenzy, shepherd, has thy soul possess'd,
Thy vineyard lies half prun'd, and half undress'd.
Quench, Corydon, thy long unanswer'd fire: 105
Mind what the common wants of life require:
On willow twigs employ thy weaving care;
And find an easier love, tho' not so fair.

VIRGIL's
PASTORALS.

PASTORAL III.

THE
ARGUMENT.

Dametas and Menalcas, after some smart strokes of country raillery, resolve to try who has the most skill at a song; and accordingly make their neighbour Palamon judge of their performances: who after a full hearing of both parties, declares himself unfit for the decision of so weighty a controversy, and leaves the victory undetermined.

THE THIRD PASTORAL.

OR,

PALÆMON.

MENALCAS, DAMÆTAS, PALÆMON.

MENALCAS.

HO, swains, what shepherd owns those ragged sheep?

DAMÆTAS.

Ægon's they are, he gave them me to keep.

MENALCAS.

Unhappy sheep of an unhappy swain!
While he Neæra courts, but courts in vain,
And fears that I the damsel shall obtain, 5
Thou, varlet, dost thy master's gains devour:
Thou milk'st his ewes, and often twice an hour;

Of grass and fodder thou defraud'st the dams;
And of their mother's dugs, the starving lambs.

DAMÆTAS.

Good words, young Catamite, at least to men: 10
We know who did your business, how, and when.
And in what chapel too you plaid your prize;
And what the goats observ'd with leering eyes:
The nymphs were kind, and laugh'd, and there
    your safety lies.

MENALCAS.

Yes, when I cropt the hedges of the Leis; 15
Cut Micon's tender vines, and stole the stays.

DAMÆTAS.

Or rather, when beneath yon ancient oak,
The bow of Daphnis, and the shafts you broke:
When the fair boy receiv'd the gift of right;
And, but for mischief, you had dy'd for spite. 20

MENALCAS.

What nonsense wou'd the fool thy master prate,
When thou, his knave, canst talk at such a rate:
Did I not see you, rascal, did I not?
When you lay snug to snap young Damon's goat?

His mungrel bark'd, I ran to his relief, 25
And cry'd, There, there he goes; stop, stop the
    thief!
Discover'd and defeated of your prey,
You skulk'd behind the fence, and sneak'd away.

DAMÆTAS.

An honest man may freely take his own;
The goat was mine, by singing fairly won. 30
A solemn match was made; he lost the prize.
Ask Damon, ask if he the debt denies;
I think he dares not; if he does he lyes.

MENALCAS.

Thou sing with him, thou booby! never pipe
Was so prophan'd to touch that blubber'd lip: 35
Dunce at the best; in streets but scarce allow'd
To tickle, on thy straw, the stupid crowd.

DAMÆTAS.

To bring it to the trial will you dare
Our pipes, our skill, our voices to compare?
My brinded heifer to the stake I lay;
Two thriving calves she suckles twice a day:

And twice besides her beestings never fail
To store the dairy with a brimming pail.
Now back your singing with an equal stake.

MENALCAS.

That should be seen, if I had one to make. 45
You know too well I feed my father's flock:
What can I wager from the common stock?
A stepdame too I have, a cursed she,
Who rules my hen-peck'd sire, and orders me.
Both number twice a-day the milky dams; 50
At once she takes the tale of all the lambs.
But since you will be mad, and since you may
Suspect my courage, if I should not lay;
The pawn I proffer shall be full as good:
Two bowls I have, well turn'd, of beechen
  wood; 55
Both by divine Alcimedon were made;
To neither of them yet the lip is laid;
The lids are ivy, grapes in clusters lurk
Beneath the carving of the curious work.
Two figures on the sides embofs'd appear; 60
Conon, and, what's his name who made the
  sphere,
And shew'd the seasons of the sliding year,

Instructed in his trade the lab'ring swain,
And when to reap, and when to sow the grain?

DAMÆTAS.

And I have two, to match your pair, at home; 65
The wood the same, from the same hand they
 come:
The kimbo handles seem with bears-foot carv'd;
And never yet to table have been serv'd:
Where Orpheus on his lyre laments his love,
With beasts encompass'd, and a dancing grove: 70
But these, not all the proffers you can make,
Are worth the heifer which I set to stake.

MENALCAS.

No more delays, vain boaster, but begin,
I prophesy before-hand I shall win.
Palæmon shall be judge how ill you rhime: 75
I'll teach you how to brag another time.

DAMÆTAS.

Rhymer come on, and do the worst you can;
I fear not you, nor yet a better man.
With silence, neighbour, and attention wait:
For 'tis a business of a high debate. 80

PALEMON.

Sing then; the shade affords a proper place;
The trees are cloath'd with leaves, the fields
    with grass;
The blossoms blow; the birds on bushes sing;
And nature has accomplish'd all the spring.
The challenge to Damætas shall belong,   85
Menalcas shall sustain his under-song:
Each in his turn your tuneful numbers bring;
By turns the tuneful Muses love to sing.

DAMÆTAS.

From the great Father of the gods above
My muse begins; for all is full of Jove;   90
T'o Jove the care of heav'n and earth belongs;
My flocks he blesses, and he loves my songs.

MENALCAS.

Me Phœbus loves; for he my muse inspires;
And in her songs, the warmth he gave, requires.
For him the God of shepherds and their sheep,   95
My blushing hyacinths, and my bays I keep.

DAMÆTAS.

My Phillis, me with pelted apples plies,
Then tripping to the woods the wanton hies;
And wishes to be seen, before she flies.

MENALCAS.

But fair Amyntas comes unask'd to me,   100
And offers love; and sits upon my knee:
Not Delia to my dogs is known so we'l as he.

DAMÆTAS.

To the dear mistress of my love-sick mind,
Her swain a pretty present has design'd:
I saw two stock-doves billing, and ere long   105
Will take the nest, and hers shall be the young.

MENALCAS.

Ten ruddy wildings in the wood I found,
And stood on tip-toes, reaching from the ground;
I sent Amyntas all my present store;
And will, to-morrow, send as many more.   110

DAMÆTAS.

The lovely maid lay panting in my arms;
And all she said and did was full of charms.

Winds on your wings to heav'n her accents bear!
Such words as heav'n alone is fit to hear.

MENALCAS.

Ah! what avails it me my love's delight, 115
To call you mine, when absent from my sight!
I hold the nets, while you pursue the prey;
And must not share the dangers of the day.

DAMÆTAS.

I keep my birth-day: send my Phyllis home;
At sheering-time, Iolas, you may come. 120

MENALCAS.

With Phyllis I am more in grace than you:
Her sorrow did my parting steps pursue:
Adieu, my dear, she said, a long adieu!

DAMÆTAS.

The nightly wolf is baneful to the fold,
Storms to the wheat, to buds the bitter cold; 125
But from my frowning fair, more ills I find
Than from the wolves, and storms, and winter-wind.

MENALCAS.

The kids with pleasure browse the bushy plain,
The show'rs are grateful to the swelling grain:
To teeming ewes the fallow's tender tree;   130
But more than all the world my love to me.

DAMÆTAS.

Pollio my rural verse vouchsafes to read:
A heifer, Muses, for your patron breed.

MENALCAS.

My Pollio writes himself, a bull be bred
With spurning heels, and with a butting head, 135
Who Pollio loves, and who his muse admires.

DAMÆTAS.

Let Pollio's fortune crown his full desires,
Let myrrh instead of thorn his fences fill;
And show'rs of honey from his oaks distil.

MENALCAS.

Who hates not living Bavius, let him be   140
(Dead Mævius) damn'd to love thy works and
        thee:
The same ill taste of sense would serve to join
Dog-foxes in the yoke, and sheer the swine.

DAMÆTAS.

Ye boys who pluck the flow'rs, and spoil the
    spring,
Beware the secret snake that shoots a sting.   145

MENALCAS.

Graze not too near the banks, my jolly sheep,
The ground is false, the running streams are
    deep:
See, they have caught the father of the flock,
Who drys his fleece upon the neigh'bring rock.

DAMÆTAS.

From rivers drive the kids, and fling your hook;
Anon I'll wash 'em in the shallow brook.   150

MENALCAS.

To fold, my flock; when milk is dry'd with
    heat,
In vain the milk-maid tugs an empty teat.

DAMÆTAS.

How lank my bulls from plenteous pasture come!
But love that drains the herd, destroys the
    groom.   155

MENALCAS.

My flocks are free from love; yet look so thin,
Their bones are barely cover'd with their skin.
What magic has bewitch'd the wooly dams,
And what ill eyes beheld the tender lambs?

DAMÆTAS.

Say, where the round of heav'n which all
    contains,   160
To three short ells on earth our sight restrains:
Tell that, and rise a Phœbus for thy pains.

MENALCAS.

Nay, tell me first, in what new region springs
A flow'r that bears inscrib'd the names of kings:
And thou shalt gain a present as divine   165
As Phœbus' self; for Phyllis shall be thine.

PALEMON.

So nice a diff'rence in your singing lies,
That both have won, or both deserv'd the prize.
Rest equal happy both; and all who prove
The bitter sweets, and pleasing pains of love. 170
Now dam the ditches, and the floods restrain:
Their moisture has already drench'd the plain.

VIRGIL's PASTORALS.

PASTORAL IV.

THE ARGUMENT.

The poet celebrates the birth-day of Salonius, the son of Pollio, born in the consulship of his father, after the taking of Solonæ, a city in Dalmatia. Many of the verses are translated from one of the Sybils, who prophesied of our Saviour's birth.

THE
FOURTH PASTORAL,
OR,
POLLIO.

SICILIAN Muse, begin a loftier strain!
    Tho' lowly shrubs and trees that shade the plain,
Delight not all; Sicilian Muse, prepare
To make the vocal woods deserve a consul's care.
The last great age, foretold by sacred rhymes,   5
Renews its finish'd course; Saturnian times
Roll round again, and mighty years, begun
From their first orb, in radiant circles run.
The base degenerate iron offspring ends;
A golden progeny from heav'n descends: 10

O chaste Lucina, speed the mother's pains;
And haste the glorious birth; thy own Apollo
  reigns!
The lovely boy, with his auspicious face,
Shall Pollio's consulship and triumph grace;
Majestic months set out with him to their ap-
  pointed race.   15
The father banish'd virtue shall restore,
And crimes shall threat the guilty world no
  more.
The son shall lead the life of gods, and be
By gods and heroes seen, and gods and heroes see.
The jarring nations he in peace shall bind,   20
And with paternal virtues rule mankind.
Unbidden earth shall wreathing ivy bring,
And fragrant herbs (the promises of spring)
As her first off'rings to her Infant king.
The goats, with strutting dugs, shall homeward
  speed,   25
And lowing herds secure from lions feed.
His cradle shall with rising flow'rs be crown'd;
The serpent's brood shall die: the sacred ground
Shall weeds and pois'nous plants refuse to bear,
Each common bush shall Syrian roses wear,   - 30

But when heroic verse his youth shall raise,
And form it to hereditary praise;
Unlabour'd harvests shall the fields adorn,
And cluster'd grapes shall blush on every thorn.
The knotted oaks shall show'rs of honey weep, 35
And through the matted grass the liquid gold shall creep.
Yet, of old fraud some footsteps shall remain,
The merchant still shall plough the deep for gain:
Great cities shall with walls be compass'd round;
And sharpen'd shares shall vex the fruitful ground, 40
Another Typhis shall new seas explore,
Another Argos land the chiefs upon th' Iberian shore.
Another Helen other wars create,
And great Achilles urge the Trojan fate.
But when to ripen'd manhood he shall grow, 45
The greedy sailor shall the seas forego;
No keel shall cut the waves for foreign ware;
For every soil shall every product bear.

The lab'ring hind his oxen shall disjoin,
No plough shall hurt the glebe, no pruning-
    hook the vine,   50
Nor wool shall in diffembled colours shine.
But the luxurious father of the fold,
With native purple, or unborrow'd gold,
Beneath his pompous fleece shall proudly sweat;
And under Tyrian robes the lamb shall bleat.   55
The Fates, when they this happy web have spun,
Shall bless the sacred clue, and bid it smoothly run.
Mature in years, to ready honours move,
O of celestial seed! O foster son of Jove!
See, lab'ring Nature calls thee to sustain   60
The nodding frame of heav'n, and earth, and
    main;
See, to their base restor'd, earth, seas, and air,
And joyful ages from behind, in crowding ranks
    appear,
To sing thy praise, wou'd heav'n my breath pro-
    long,   65
Infusing spirits worthy such a song;
Not Thracian Orpheus should transcend my lays,
Nor Linus, crown'd with never-fading bays;

Though each his heav'nly parent should inspire;
The Muse instruct the voice, and Phœbus tune
    the lyre.   70
Shou'd Pan contend in verse, and tho my
    theme,
Arcadian judges should their God condemn.
Begin, auspicious boy, to cast about
Thy infant eyes, and, with a smile, thy mother
    single out;
Thy mother well deserves that short delight,   75
The nauseous qualms of ten long months and
    travel to requite.
Then smile; the frowning infant's doom is read,
No god shall crown the board, nor goddess bless
    the bed.

VIRGIL's PASTORALS.

PASTORAL V.

THE ARGUMENT.

Mopsus and Menalcas, two very expert shepherds at a song, begin one by consent to the memory of Daphnis; who is supposed, by the best critics, to represent Julius Cæsar. Mopsus laments his death, Menalcas proclaims his divinity: the whole Eclogue consisting of an elegy and an apotheosis.

THE FIFTH PASTORAL.

OR,

DAPHNIS.

MENALCAS.

SINCE on the downs our flocks together feed,
   And since my voice can match your tuneful reed,
Why sit we not beneath the grateful shade,
Which hazles, intermix'd with elms, have made?

MOPSUS.

  Whether you please that silvan scene to take,   5
Where whistling winds uncertain shadows make:
Or will you to the cooler cave succeed,
Whose mouth the curling vines have overspread?

MENALCAS.

Your merit and your years command the choice:
Amyntas only rivals you in voice. .   10

MOPSUS.

What will not that presuming shepherd dare,
Who thinks his voice with Phœbus may compare?

MENALCAS.

Begin you first; if either Alcon's praise,
Or dying Phyllis have inspir'd your lays:
If her you mourn, or Codrus you commend,   15
Begin, and Tityrus your flock shall tend.

MOPSUS.

Or shall I rather the sad verse repeat,
Which on the beeches' bark I lately writ:
I writ, and sung betwixt; now bring the swain
Whose voice you boast, and let him try the strain. 20

MENALCAS.

Such as the shrub to the tall olive shows,
Or the pale sallow to the blushing rose;
Such is his voice, if I can judge aright,
Compar'd to thine, in sweetness and in height.

MOPSUS.

  No more, but sit and hear the promis'd lay,   25
The gloomy grotto makes a doubtful day.
The nymphs about the breathless body wait
Of Daphnis, and lament his cruel fate.
The trees and floods were witness to their tears:
At length — rumour reach'd his mother's ears.   30
The wretched parent, with —,
Came running, and his lifeless limbs embrac'd.
She sigh'd, she sob'd, and, furious with despair,
She rent her garments, and she tore her hair:
Accusing all the gods, and every star.   35
The swains forgot their sheep, nor near the brink
Of running waters brought their herds to drink.
The thirsty cattle, of themselves, abstain'd
From water, and their grassy fare disdain'd.
The death of Daphnis woods and hills deplore,   40
They cast the sound to Lybia's desert shore;
The Lybian lions hear, and hearing roar.
Fierce tigers Daphnis taught the yoke to bear;
And first with curling ivy dress'd the spear:
Daphnis did rites to Bacchus first ordain;   45
And holy revels for his reeling train.

As vines the trees, as grapes the vines adorn,
As bulls the herds, and fields the yellow corn;
So bright a splendor, so divine a grace,
The glorious Daphnis cast on his illustrious race. 50
When envious fate the godlike Daphnis took,
Our guardian gods the fields and plains forsook:
Pales no longer swelled the teeming grain,
Nor Phoebus fed his oxen on the plain;
No fruitful crop the sickly fields return; 55
But oats and darnel choak the rising corn.
And where the vales with violets once were crown'd,
Now knotty burrs and thorns disgrace the ground.
Come, shepherds, come, and strow with leaves the
 plain;
Such funeral rites your Daphnis did ordain. 60
With cypress boughs the crystal fountains hide,
And softly let the running waters glide;
A lasting monument to Daphnis raise,
With this inscription to record his praise:
Daphnis, the field's delight, the shepherd's love, 65
Renown'd on earth, and deify'd above;
Whose flock excell'd the fairest on the plains,
But less than he himself surpass'd the swains.

MENALCAS.

O heav'nly poet! such thy verse appears,
So sweet, so charming to my ravish'd ears, 70
As to the weary swain, with cares opprest,
Beneath the sylvan shade, refreshing rest:
As to the fev'rish traveller, when first
He finds a crystal stream to quench his thirst.
In singing, as in piping, you excel; 75
And scarce your master could perform so well.
O fortunate young man, at least your lays
Are next to his, and claim the second praise.
Such as they are, my rural songs I join,
To raise our Daphnis to the pow'rs divine; 80
For Daphnis was so good, to love what'er was mine.

MOPSUS.

How is my soul with such a promise rais'd!
For both the boy was worthy to be prais'd,
And Stimichon has often made me long
To hear like him, so sof, so sweet a song. 85

MENALCAS.

Daphnis, the guest of heav'n, with won'dring eyes,
Views in the milky way the starry skies.

And far beneath him, from the shining sphere,
Beholds the moving clouds, and rolling year.
For this, with chearful cries the woods resound; 90
The purple spring arrays the various ground;
The nymphs and shepherds dance; and Pan
    himself is crown'd.
The wolf no longer prowls for nightly spoils,
Nor birds the sprindges fear, nor stags the toils:
For Daphnis reigns above; and deals from
    thence   95
His mother's milder beams, and peaceful influence.
The mountain-tops unshorn, the rocks rejoice;
The lowly shrubs partake of human voice.
Assenting Nature, with a gracious nod,
Proclaims him, and salutes the new admitted
    God.   100
Be still propitious, ever good to thine;
Behold four hallow'd altars we design;
And two to thee, and two to Phœbus rise;
On both are offer'd annual sacrifice.
The holy priests, at each returning year, 105
Two bowls of milk, and two of oil shall bear;
And I myself the guests with friendly bowls
    will cheer.

Two goblets will I crown with sparkling wine,
The gen'rous vintage of the Chian vine;
These will I pour to thee, and make the nectar
    thine.   110
In winter shall the genial feast be made
Before the fire; by summer in the shade.
Dametas shall perform the rites divine;
And Lictian Ægon in the song shall join,
Alphesibeus, tripping, shall advance;   115
And mimic satyrs in his antic dance.
When to the nymphs our annual rites we pay,
And when our fields with victims we survey:
While savage boars delight in shady woods,
And finny fish inhabit in the floods;   120
While bees on thyme, and locusts feed on dew,
Thy grateful swains these honours shall renew.
Such honours as we pay to Pow'rs divine,
To Bacchus and to Ceres shall be thine.
Such annual honours shall be giv'n, and thou   125
Shalt hear, and shalt condemn thy suppliants to
    their vow.

MOPSUS.

What present worth thy verse can Mopsus find!
Not the soft whispers of a southern wind,

That play through trembling trees, delight me
    more;
Nor murm'ring billows on the founding fhore; 130
Nor winding ſtreams that through the valley glide;
And the ſcarce-covered pebbles gently chide.

MENALCAS.

Receive you firſt this tuneful pipe; the fame
That play'd my Corydon's unhappy flame.
The ſame that ſung Neæra's conqu'ring eyes; 135
And, had the judge been juſt, had won the prize.

MOPSUS.

Accept from me this ſheephook, in exchange,
The handle braſs; the knobs in equal range,
Antigenes, with kiſſes, often try'd
To beg this preſent, in his beauty's pride; 140
When youth and love are hard to be deny'd.
But what I could refuſe to his requeſt,
Is yours unaſk'd, for you deſerve it beſt.

VIRGIL's
PASTORALS.

PASTORAL VI.

THE ARGUMENT.

Two young shepherds, Chromis and Mnasylus, having been promis'd a song by Silenus, chance to catch him asleep in this Pastoral; where they bind him hand and foot, and then claim his promise. Silenus finding they would be put off no longer, begins his song, in which he describes the formation of the universe, and the original of animals, according to the Epicurean philosophy; and then runs through the most surprizing transformations which have happened in nature since her birth. This Pastoral was designed as a compliment to Syro the Epicurean, who instructed Virgil and Varus in the principles of that philosophy. Silenus acts as tutor, Chromis and Mnasylus as the two pupils.

THE SIXTH PASTORAL.

OR,

SILENUS.

I FIRST transferr'd to Rome Sicilian strains:
  Nor blush'd the Doric Muse to dwell on
    Mantuan plains.
But when I try'd her tender voice, too young,
And fighting kings, and bloody battles sung;
Apollo check'd my pride, and bade me feed   5
My fat'ning flocks, nor dare beyond the reed.
Admonish'd thus, while every pen prepares
To write thy praises, Varus, and thy wars,
My past'ral Muse her humble tribute brings;
And yet not wholly uninspired she sings.   10

For all who read, and reading not disdain
These rural poems, and their lowly strain,
The name of Varus, oft inscrib'd shall see,
In every grove, and every vocal tree;
And all the sylvan reign shall sing of thee: 15
Thy name, to Phœbus and the Muses known,
Shall in the front of every page be shown;
For he who sings thy praise, secures his own.
Proceed, my Muse: Two satyrs, on the ground,
Stretch'd at his ease, their sire Silenus found. 20
Dos'd with his fumes, and heavy with his load,
They found him snoring in his dark abode;
And seiz'd with youthful arms the drunken God.
His rosy wreath was dropt not long before,
Borne by the tide of wine, and floating on the
  floor. 25
His empty can, with ears half worn away,
Was hung on high, to boast the triumph of the
  day.
Invaded thus, for want of better bands,
His garland they unstring, and bind his hands:
For by the fraudful God deluded long, 30
They now resolve to have their promis'd song.

VI. Part Vol 3 p 160

Ægle came in, to make their party good;
The faireſt Naïs of the neighbouring flood,
And, while he ſtares around with ſtupid eyes,
His brows with berries, and his temples dyes.   35
He finds the fraud, and, with a ſmile, demands
On what deſign the boy had bound his hands.
Looſe me, he cry'd; 'twas impudence to find
A ſleeping God, 'tis ſacrilege to bind.
To you the promis'd poem I will pay;   40
The nymph ſhall be rewarded in her way.
He rais'd his voice; and ſoon a num'rous throng
Of tripping ſatyrs crowded to the ſong;
And ſylvan fauns, and ſavage beaſts advanc'd,
And nodding foreſts to the numbers danc'd.   45
Not by Hæmonian hills the Thracian bard,
Nor awful Phœbus was on Pindus heard,
With deeper ſilence or with more regard.
He ſung the ſecret ſeeds of nature's frame;
How ſeas, and earth, and air, and active flame, 50
Fell through the mighty void, and in their fall
Were blindly gather'd in this goodly ball.

The tender soil then stiff'ning by degrees,
Shut from the bounded earth, the bounding
    seas.
Then earth and ocean various forms disclose;
And a new sun to the new world arose.   55
And mists condens'd to clouds obscure the sky;
And clouds dissolv'd, the thirsty ground supply.
The rising trees the lofty mountains grace:
The lofty mountains feed the savage race,   60
Yet few, and strangers, in th' unpeopled place.
From thence the birth of man the song pursu'd,
And how the world was lost, and how renew'd.
The reign of Saturn, and the golden age;
Prometheus' theft, and Jove's avenging rage.   65
The cries of Argonauts for Hylas drown'd;
With whose repeated name the shores resound.
Then mourns the madness of the Cretan queen:
Happy for her if herds had never been.
What fury, wretched woman, seiz'd thy
    breast?   70
The maids of Argos (tho' with rage possess'd,
Their imitated lowings fill'd the grove)
Yet shun'd the guilt of thy prepost'rous love,

Nor sought the youthful husband of the herd,
Tho' labring yokes on their own necks they
    fear'd;   75
And felt for budding horns on their smooth
    foreheads rear'd.
Ah, wretched queen! you range the pathless
    wood;
While on a flowry bank he chews the cud:
Or sleeps in shades, or thro' the forest roves;
And roars with anguish for his absent loves.   80
Ye nymphs, with toils his forest-walk sur-
    round;
And trace his wand'ring footsteps on the ground.
But, ah! perhaps my passion he disdains;
And courts the milky mothers of the plains.
We search th'ungrateful fugitive abroad;   85
While they at home sustain his happy load.
He sung the lover's fraud; the longing maid,
With golden fruit, like all the sex, betray'd:
The sister's mourning for the brother's loss;
Their bodies hid in barks, and fur'd with moss. 90
How each a rising alder now appears:
And o'er the Po distils her gummy tears.

Then sung, how Gallus by a Muse's hand
Was led and welcom'd to the sacred strand.
The senate rising to salute their guest;   95
And Linus thus their gratitude express'd,
Receive this present by the Muses made;
The pipe on which th' Ascræan pastor play'd;
With which of old he charm'd the savage train,
And call'd the mountain ashes to the plain.   100
Sing thou on this, thy Phœbus; and the wood
Where once his fane of Parian marble stood.
On this his ancient oracles rehearse:
And with new numbers grace the god of verse.
Why should I sing the double Scylla's fate,   105
The first by love transform'd, the last by hate.
A beauteous maid above, but magic arts
With barking dogs deform'd her nether parts:
What vengeance on the passing fleet she pour'd,
The master frighted, and the mates devour'd.   100
Then ravish'd Philomel the song express;
The crime reveal'd; the sisters cruel feast:
And how in fields the lapwing Tereus reigns
The warbling nightingale in woods complains.

While Progne makes, on chimney-tops her
    moan; 115
And hovers o'er the palace once her own.
Whatever songs besides, the Delphian God
Had taught the laurels, and the Spartan flood,
Silenus sung: the vales his voice rebound,
And carry to the skies the sacred sound. 120
And now the setting sun had warn'd the swain
To call his counted cattle from the plain:
Yet still th' unweary'd sire pursues the tuneful
    strain.
Till unperceiv'd the heav'ns with stars were hung:
And sudden night surpriz'd the yet unfinish'd
    song. 125

VIRGIL's PASTORALS.

PASTORAL VII.

THE ARGUMENT.

Melibœus here gives us the relation of a sharp poetical contest between Thyrsis and Corydon; at which he himself and Daphnis were present; who hath declared for Corydon.

THE

SEVENTH PASTORAL.

OR,

MELIBŒUS.

Beneath a holm, repair'd two jolly swains;
  Their sheep and goats together graz'd the plains;
Both young Arcadians, both alike inspir'd
To sing, and answer as the song requir'd.
Daphnis, as umpire, took the middle seat;   5
And fortune thither led my weary feet.
For while I fenc'd my myrtles from the cold,
The father of my flock had wander'd from the fold.
Of Daphnis I enquir'd; he, smiling, said,
Dismiss your fear, and pointed where he fed.   10

And, if no greater cares disturb your mind,
Sit here with us, in covert of the wind.
Your lowing heifers, of their own accord,
At wat'ring time will seek the neighb'ring ford.
Here wanton Mincius winds along the meads, 15
And shades his happy banks with bending reeds:
And see from yon old oak, that mates the skies,
How black the clouds of swarming bees arise.
What shou'd I do! nor was Alcippe nigh,
Nor absent Phyllis cou'd my care supply, 20
To house and feed by hand my weaning lambs,
And drain the strutting udders of their dams?
Great was the strife betwixt the singing swains:
And I preferr'd my pleasure to my gains.
Alternate rhyme the ready champions chose: 25
These Corydon rehears'd, and Thyrsis those.

CORYDON.

Ye Muses, ever fair, and ever young,
Assist my numbers, and inspire my song.
With all my Codrus O inspire my breast,
For Codrus, after Phœbus, sings the best. 30
Or if my wishes have presum'd too high,
And stretch'd their bounds beyond mortality,

The praise of artful numbers I resign:
And hang my pipe upon the sacred pine.

THYRSIS.

Arcadian swains, your youthful poet crown 35
With ivy wreaths; tho' surly Codrus frown.
Or if he blast my Muse with envious praise,
Then fence my brows with amulets of bays;
Lest his ill arts or his malicious tongue
Shou'd poison, or bewitch my growing song. 40

CORYDON.

These branches of a stag, this tusky boar
(The first essay of arms untry'd before)
Young Mycon offers, Delia, to thy shrine;
But speed his hunting with thy pow'r divine.
Thy statue then of Parian stone shall stand; 45
Thy legs in buskins with a purple band.

THYRSIS.

This bowl of milk, these cakes, (our country
    fare,)
For thee, Priapus, yearly we prepare,
Because a little garden is thy care.

But if the falling lambs increase my fold, 50
Thy marble statue shall be turn'd to gold.

CORYDON.

Fair Galatea, with thy silver feet,
O, whiter than the swan, and more than Hybla
    sweet;
Tall as a poplar, taper as the bole,
Come charm thy shepherd, and restore my soul. 55
Come when my lated sheep at night return;
And crown the silent hours, and stop the rosy morn.

THYRSIS.

May I become as abject in thy sight,
As sea-weed on the shore, and black as night:
Rough as a bur, deform'd like him who chaws 60
Sardinian herbage to contract his jaws;
Such and so monstrous let thy swain appear,
If one day's absence looks not like a year.
Hence from the field for shame: the flock deserves
No better feeding, while the shepherd starves. 65

CORYDON.

Ye mossy springs, inviting easy sleep,
Ye trees, whose leafy shades those mossy fountains
    keep,

Defend my flock; the summer heats are near,
And blossoms on the swelling vines appear.

THYRSIS.

With heapy fires our chearful hearth is crown'd; 70
And firs for torches in the woods abound:
We fear not more the winds, and wintry cold,
Than streams the banks, or wolves the bleating fold.

CORYDON.

Our woods with juniper and chesnuts crown'd,
With falling fruits and berries paint the ground;
And lavish nature laughs, and strows her stores around. 76
But if Alexis from our mountains fly,
Ev'n running rivers leave their channels dry.

THYRSIS.

Parch'd are the plains, and frying is the field,
Nor with'ring vines their juicy vintage yield. 80
But if returning Phyllis bless the plain,
The grass revives; the woods are green again;
And Jove descends in show'rs of kindly rain.

CORYDON.

The poplar is by great Alcides worn;
The brows of Phœbus his own bays adorn;　　85
The branching vine the jolly Bacchus loves;
The Cyprian queen delights in myrtle groves.
With hazle Phyllis crowns her flowing hair;
And while she loves that common wreath to wear,
Nor bays, nor myrtle boughs, with hazle shall
　　compare.　　　　　　　　　　　　　　90

THYRSIS.

The tow'ring ash is fairest in the woods;
In gardens pines, and poplars by the floods:
But if my Lycidas will ease my pains,
And often visit our forsaken plains,
To him the tow'ring ash shall yield in woods;　95
In gardens pines, and poplars by the floods.

MELIBŒUS.

These rhymes I did to memory commend,
When vanquish'd Thyrsis did in vain contend;
Since when, 'tis Corydon among the swains,
Young Corydon without a rival reigns.　　100

VIRGIL's PASTORALS.

PASTORAL VIII.

THE ARGUMENT.

This Pastoral contains the songs of Damon and Alphesibœus. The first of them bewails the loss of his mistress, and repines at the success of his rival Mopsus. The other repeats the charms of some enchantress, who endeavoured by her spells and magic to make Daphnis in love with her.

THE

EIGHTH PASTORAL,

OR,

PHARMACEUTRIA;

THE mournful Muse of two despairing swains,
The love rejected, and the lover's pains,
To which the savage lynxes list'ning stood,
The rivers stood on heaps, and stopp'd the running flood:
The hungry herd their needful food refuse;   5
Of two despairing swains, I sing the mournful muse.
  Great Pollio, thou for whom thy Rome prepares
The ready triumph of thy finish'd wars,

Whether Timavus or th' Illyrian coast,
Whatever land or sea thy presence boast; 10
Is there an hour in fate reserv'd for me,
To sing thy deeds in numbers worthy thee?
In numbers like to thine, could I rehearse
Thy lofty tragic scenes, thy labour'd verse:
The world another Sophocles in thee, 15
Another Homer shou'd behold in me:
Amidst thy laurels let this ivy twine,
Thine was my earliest Muse; my latest shall be
    thine.

  Scarce from the world the shades of night with-
    drew; 19
Scarce were the flocks refresh'd with morning dew,
When Damon stretch'd beneath an olive shade,
And wildly staring upwards, thus inveigh'd
Against the conscious gods, and curs'd the cruel
    maid:
Star of the morning, why dost thou delay?
Come, Lucifer, drive on the lagging day; 25
While I my Nisa's perjur'd faith deplore;
Witness ye Pow'rs, by whom she falsely swore!

The Gods, alas, are witnesses in vain;
Yet shall my dying breath to heav'n complain.
Begin with me, my flute, the sweet Mænalian
    strain.   30

  The pines of Mænalus, the vocal grove,
Are ever full of verse, and full of love:
They hear the hinds, they hear their God com-
    plain;
Who suffer'd not the reeds to rise in vain.
Begin with me, my flute, the sweet Mænalian
    strain.   35

  Mopsus triumphs; he weds the willing fair:
When such is Nisa's choice, what lover can de-
    spair!
Now griffons join with mares, another age
Shall see the hound and hind their thirst assuage
Promiscuous at the spring: prepare the lights,   40
O Mopsus! and perform the bridal rites.
Scatter thy nuts among the scrambling boys:
Thine is the night, and thine the nuptial joys.
For thee the sun declines, O happy swain!
Begin with me, my flute, the sweet Mænalian
    strain.

I 4

O, Nisa! justly to thy choice condemn'd!
Whom hast thou taken, whom hast thou con-
　　temn'd;
For him, thou hast refus'd my browsing herd,
Scorn'd my thick eye-brows, and my shaggy beard.
Unhappy Damon sighs, and sings in vain: 　50
While Nisa thinks no God regards a lover's pain.
Begin with me, my flute, the sweet Mænalian
　　strain.

　I view'd thee first, how fatal was the view!
And led thee where the ruddy wildings grew,
High on the planted hedge, and wet with morn-
　　ing dew. 　　　　　　　　.　　55
Then scarce the bending branches I cou'd win;
The callow down began to cloath my chin;
I saw, I perish'd, yet indulg'd my pain:
Begin with me, my flute, the sweet Mænalian
　　strain.

　I know thee, love, in deserts thou wert bred, 60
And at the dugs of savage tigers fed:
Alien of birth, usurper of the plains,
Begin with me, my flute, the sweet Mænalian
　　strains.

Relentless love the cruel mother led,
The blood of her unhappy babes to shed: 65
Love lent the sword, the mother struck the blow,
Inhuman she, but more inhuman thou:
Alien of birth, usurper of the plains,
Begin with me, my flute, the sweet Mænalian
    strains.

Old doting nature, change thy course anew, 70
And let the trembling lamb the wolf pursue:
Let oaks now glitter with Hesperian fruit,
And purple daffodils from alder shoot.
Fat amber let the tamarisk distil,
And hooting owls contend with swans in skill. 75
Hoarse Tityrus strive with Orpheus in the woods,
And challenge fam'd Arion on the floods.
Or, oh! let nature cease, and chaos reign,
Begin with me, my flute, the sweet Mænalian
    strain.

Let earth be sea, and let the whelming tide 80
The lifeless limbs of luckless Damon hide:
Farewel, ye secret woods, and shady groves,
Haunts of my youth, and conscious of my loves!

From yon high cliff I plunge into the main,
Take the last present of thy dying swain,   85
And cease, my silent flute, the sweet Mænalian
    strain.

Now take your turns, ye Muses, to rehearse
His friend's complaints, and mighty magic verse:
Bring running water, bind those altars round
With fillets, and with vervain strow the ground: 90
Make fat with frankincense the sacred fires,
To re-inflame my Daphnis with desires:
'Tis done, we want but verse. Restore my
    charms,
My ling'ring Daphnis to my longing arms.

  Pale Phœbe, drawn by verse from heav'n de-
    scends,   95
And Circe chang'd with charms Ulysses' friends.
Verse breaks the ground, and penetrates the
    brake,
And in the winding cavern splits the snake.
Verse fires the frozen veins; restore, my charms,
My ling'ring Daphnis to my longing arms.   100

Around his waxen image first I wind
Three woollen fillets, of three colours join'd:
Thrice bind about his thrice-devoted head,
Which round the sacred altar thrice is led:
Unequal numbers please the Gods: my charms, 105
Restore my Daphnis to my longing arms.

Knit with three knots the fillets, knit 'em
straight;
Then say, these knots to love I consecrate.
Haste, Amaryllis, haste, restore my charms,
My lovely Daphnis to my longing arms. 110

As fire this figure hardens, made of clay;
And this of wax with fire consumes away;
Such let the soul of cruel Daphnis be,
Hard to the rest of women, soft to me:
Crumble the sacred mole of salt and corn, 115
Next in the fire the bays with brimstone burn.
And while it crackles in the sulphur, say,
This, I for Daphnis burn; thus Daphnis burn
away.

This laurel is his fate; restore, my charms,
My lovely Daphnis to my longing arms.   120

    As when the raging heifer, through the grove,
Stung with desire, pursues her wand'ring love;
Faint at the last, she seeks the weedy pools
To quench her thirst, and on the rushes rolls:
Careless of night, unmindful to return,   125
Such fruitless fires perfidious Daphnis burn.
While I so scorn his love, restore, my charms,
My ling'ring Daphnis to my longing arms.

    These garments once were his, and left to me
The pledges of his promis'd loyalty;   130
Which underneath my threshold I bestow
These pawns, O sacred earth! to me my Daphnis
    owe.
As these were his, so mine is he, my charms,
Restore their ling'ring lord to my deluded arms.

    These pois'nous plants, for magic use de-
    sign'd,   135
(The noblest and the best of all the baneful kind)

Old Mœris brought me from the Pontic strand,
And cull'd the mischief of a bounteous land.
Smear'd with these pow'rful juices, on the plain
He howls a wolf among the hungry train: 140
And oft the mighty necromancer boasts,
With these, to call from tombs the stalking ghosts,
And from the roots to tear the standing corn,
Which, whirl'd aloft, to distant fields is born.
Such is the strength of spells; restore, my charms,   145
My ling'ring Daphnis to my longing arms.

Bear out these ashes, cast 'em in the brook,
Cast backwards o'er your head, nor turn your look,
Since neither gods, nor godlike verse can move,
Break out ye smother'd fires, and kindle smother'd love.   150
Exert your utmost pow'r, my ling'ring charms,
And force my Daphnis to my longing arms.

See, while my last endeavours I delay,
The waking ashes rise, and round our altars play!

Run to the threshold, Amaryllis; hark, 155
Our Hylas opens, and begins to bark.
Good heav'n! may lovers what they wish believe,
Or dream their wishes, and those dreams deceive!
No more, my Daphnis comes; no more, my charms,
He comes, he runs, he leaps, to my desiring arms. 160

VIRGIL's
PASTORALS.

PASTORAL IX.

THE ARGUMENT.

When Virgil, by the favour of Augustus, had recovered his patrimony near Mantua, and went in hope to take possession, he was in danger to be slain by Arius the centurion, to whom those lands were assigned by the emperor, in reward of his service against Brutus and Cassius. This Pastoral therefore is filled with complaints of his hard usage; and the persons introduced are the bailiff of Virgil Mœris, and his friend Lycidas.

THE NINTH PASTORAL;

OR,

LYCIDAS AND MŒRIS.

LYCIDAS.

Ho, Mœris! whither on thy way so fast?
This leads to town.

MŒRIS.

O Lycidas, at last
The time is come I never thought to see,
(Strange revolution for my farm and me)
When the grim captain in a surly tone
Cries out, pack up, ye rascals! and be gone.

Kick'd out, we set the best face on't we cou'd,
And these two kids t'appease his angry mood
I bear, of which the Furies give him good.   10

LYCIDAS.

Your country friends were told another tale,
That from the sloping mountain to the vale,
And dodder'd oak, and all the banks along,
Menalcas sav'd his fortune with a song.

MŒRIS.

Such was the news, indeed; but songs and
    rhymes   15
Prevail as much in these hard iron times,
As would a plump of trembling fowl, that rise
Against an eagle sousing from the skies:
And had not Phœbus warn'd me by the croak
Of an old raven, from a hollow oak;   20
To shun debate, Menalcas had been slain,
And Mœris not surviv'd him, to complain.

LYCIDAS.

Now heav'n defend! cou'd barb'rous rage induce
The brutal son of Mars t'insult the sacred Muse!

Who then should sing the nymphs, or who re-
    hearse   25.
The waters gliding in a smoother verse!
Or Amaryllis praise, that heav'nly lay
That shorten'd, as we went, our tedious way.
O Tityrus, tend my herd, and see them fed,
To morning pastures, evening waters led;   30
And 'ware the Libyan ridgel's butting head.

MŒRIS.

Or what unfinish'd he to Varus read;
Thy name, O Varus (if the kinder pow'rs
Preserve our plains, and shield the Mantuan
    tow'rs,
Obnoxious by Cremona's neighb'ring crime)   35
The wings of swans, and stronger pinion'd rhyme,
Shall raise aloft, and soaring bear above
Th' immortal gift of gratitude to Jove.

LYCIDAS.

Sing on, sing on, for I can ne'er be cloy'd,
So may thy swarms the baleful eugh avoid: 40
So may thy cows their burden'd bags distend,
And trees to goats their willing branches bend.

Mean as I am, yet have the Muses made
Me free, a member of the tuneful trade:
At least the shepherds seem to like my lays,   45
But I discern their flattery from their praise:
I nor to Cinna's ears, nor Varus dare aspire,
But gabble like a goose, amidst the swan-like
    quire.

MŒRIS.

'Tis what I have been conning in my mind,
Nor are the verses of a vulgar kind.   50
Come, Galatea, come, the seas forsake,
What pleasures can the tides with their hoarse
    murmurs make?
See, on the shore inhabits purple spring,
Where nightingales their love-sick ditty sing;
See, meads with purling streams, with flow'rs
    the ground,   55
The grottoes cool, with shady poplars crown'd,
And creeping vines on arbours weav'd around,
Come then, and leave the waves' tumultuous
    roar,
Let the wild surges vainly beat the shore.

Gen.II Vol.I p.300

J. Collyer sculp.

NAPOLI

LYCIDAS.

Or that sweet song I heard with such delight,   60
The same you sung alone one starry night;
The tune I still retain, but not the words.

MŒRIS.

Why, Daphnis, dost thou search in old records,
To know the seasons when the stars arise?
See Cæsar's lamp is lighted in the skies: 65
The star, whose rays the blushing grapes adorn,
And swell the kindly ripening ears of corn.
Under this influence, graft the tender shoot,
Thy childrens children shall enjoy the fruit.
The rest I have forgot, for cares and time   70
Change all things, and untune my soul to rhyme:
I could have once sung down a summer's sun,
But now the chime of poetry is done.
My voice grows hoarse, I feel the notes decay,
As if the wolves had seen me first to-day.   70
But these, and more than I to mind can bring,
Menalcas has not yet forgot to sing.

LYCIDAS.

Thy faint excuses but inflame me more,
And now the waves roll silent to the shore.

Hufht winds the topmaft branches fcarcely bend, 80
As if thy tuneful fong they did attend;
Already we have half our way o'ercome,
Far off I can difcern Bianor's tomb;
Here, where the labourer's hands have form'd a bow'r
Of wreathing trees, in finging wafte an hour. 85
Reft here thy weary limbs, thy kids lay down,
We've day before us yet to reach the town:
Or if ere night the gath'ring clouds we fear,
A fong will help the beating ftorm to bear:
And that thou may'ft not be too late abroad, 90
Sing, I'll eafe thy fhoulders of thy load.

MOERIS.

Ceafe to requeft me, let us mind our way,
Another fong requires another day.
When good Menalcas comes, if he rejoice,
And find a friend at court, I'll find a voice. 95

VIRGIL's PASTORALS.

PASTORAL X.

THE ARGUMENT.

Gallus, a great patron of Virgil, and an excellent poet, was very deeply in love with one Citheris, whom he calls Lycoris, and who had forsaken him for the company of a soldier. The poet therefore supposes his friend Gallus retired in his height of melancholy into the solitudes of Arcadia, (the celebrated scene of pastorals) where he represents him in a very languishing condition, with all the rural Deities about him, pitying his hard usage, and condoling his misfortune.

THE
TENTH PASTORAL;
OR,
GALLUS.

THY sacred succour, Arethusa, bring,
    To crown my labour: 'tis the last I sing.
Which proud Lycoris may with pity view,
The Muse is mournful, tho' the numbers few,
Refuse me not a verse, to grief and Gallus due.   5
So may thy silver streams beneath the tide,
Unmix'd with briny seas, securely glide.
Sing then, my Gallus, and his hopeless vows;
Sing, while my cattle crop the tender browse.
The vocal grove shall answer to the sound,   10
And echo, from the vales, the tuneful voice re-
    bound.

What lawns or woods withheld you from his aid,
Ye nymphs, when Gallus was to love betray'd;
To love, unpity'd by the cruel maid?
Nor steepy Pindus cou'd retard your course, 15
Nor cleft Parnassus, nor th' Aonian source:
Nothing that owns the Muses cou'd suspend
Your aid to Gallus, Gallus is their friend.
For him the lofty laurel stands in tears,
And hung with humid pearls the lowly shrub appears. 20
Mænalian pines the godlike swain bemoan,
When spread beneath a rock he sigh'd alone,
And cold Lycæus wept from every dropping stone.
The sheep surround their shepherd as he lies,
Blush not, sweet poet, nor the name despise; 25
Along the streams his flock Adonis fed,
And yet the queen of beauty blest his bed.
The swains and tardy neat-herds came, and last
Menalcas, wet with beating winter mast. 30
Wond'ring they ask'd from whence arose thy flame,
Yet more amaz'd, thy own Apollo came.

Flush'd were his cheeks, and glowing were his
    eyes;
Is she thy care? is she thy care? he cries.
Thy false Lycoris flies thy love and thee,
And for thy rival tempts the raging sea,   35
The forms of horrid war, and heav'n's incle-
    mency.
Sylvanus came; his brows a country crown
Of fennel, and of nodding lilies, drown.
Great Pan arriv'd, and we beheld him too,
His cheeks and temples of vermilion hue: 40
Why, Gallus, this immod'rate grief, he cry'd,
Think'st thou that love with tears is satisfy'd?
The meads are sooner drunk with morning dews,
The bees with flow'ry shrubs, the goats with
    browse.
Unmov'd and with dejected eyes he mourn'd,   45
He paus'd, and then these broken words return'd:
'Tis past; and pity gives me no relief,
But you, Arcadian swains, shall sing my grief;
And on your hills my last complaints renew,
So sad a song is only worthy you,   50
How light wou'd lie the turf upon my breast,
If you my suff'rings in your songs exprest?

Ah! that your birth and bus'ness had been mine,
To penn the sheep, and press the swelling vine!
Had Phyllis or Amyntas caus'd my pain,   55
Or any nymph, or any shepherd on the plain,
Tho' Phyllis brown, tho' black Amyntas were,
Are violets not sweet, because not fair?
Beneath the sallows and the shady vine,
My loves had mix'd their pliant limbs with mine; 60
Phyllis with myrtle wreaths had crown'd my
    hair,
And soft Amyntas sung away my care.
Come, see what pleasures in our plains abound,
The woods, the fountains, and the flow'ry ground.
As you are beauteous, were you half so true, 65
Here cou'd I live, and love, and die with only you.
Now I to fighting fields am sent afar,
And strive in winter camps with toils of war;
While you, (alas, that I should find it so!)
To shun my sight, your native soil forego,   70
And climb the frozen Alps, and tread th' eter-
    nal snow.
Ye frosts and snows her tender body spare,
Those are not limbs for isicles to tear.

For me, the wilds and defarts are my choice,
The Mufes, once my care; my once harmonious
    voice. 79
There will I fing, forfaken and alone,
The rocks and hollow caves fhall echo to my moan.
The rind of ev'ry plant her name fhall know,
And as the rind extends the love fhall grow.
Then on Arcadian mountains will I chace 80
(Mix'd with the woodland nymphs) the favage race,
Nor cold fhall hinder me, with horns and hounds
To thrid the thickets, or to leap the mounds.
And now methinks o'er fteepy rocks I go,
And rufh through founding woods, and bend the
    Parthian bow: 85
As if with fports my fufferings I could eafe,
Or by my pains the God of Love appeafe.
My frenzy changes, I delight no more
On mountain tops to chace the tufky boar:
No game but hopelefs love my thoughts purfue, 90
Once more ye nymphs, and fongs, and founding
    woods adieu.
Love alters not for us his hard decrees,
Not tho' beneath the Thracian clime we freeze;

Or Italy's indulgent heav'n forego;
And in mid-winter tread Sithonian snow: 95
Or when the barks of elms are scorch'd, we keep
On Meroe's burning plains the Libyan sheep.
In hell, and earth, and seas, and heav'n above,
Love conquers all, and we must yield to love.
My Muses, here your sacred raptures end,   100
The verse was what I ow'd my suff'ring friend.
This while I sung, my sorrows I deceiv'd,
And bending osiers into baskets weav'd.
The song, because inspir'd by you, shall shine,
And Gallus will approve, because 'tis mine: 105
Gallus, for whom my holy flames renew
Each hour, and ev'ry moment rise in view:
As alders, in the spring, their boles extend,
And heave so fiercely, that the bark they rend.
Now let us rise, for hoarseness oft invades   110
The singer's voice, who sings beneath the shades.
From juniper unwholsome dews distil,
That blast the sooty corn, the with'ring herb-
  age kill;
Away, my goats, away, for you have brows'd
  your fill.

VIRGIL's
GEORGICS.

DEDICATED TO THE

EARL OF CHESTERFIELD.

To the Right Honourable

P H I L I P

EARL of CHESTERFIELD, &c.

My Lord,

I Cannot begin my address to your Lordship, better than in the words of Virgil,

—Quod obtanti, Divûm promittere nemo
Auderet, volvendo dies, en, attulit ultro.

Seven years together I have concealed the longing which I had to appear before you: a time as tedious as Æneas passed in his wandering voyage, before he reached the promised Italy. But I considered, that nothing which my meanness could produce was worthy of your patronage: At last this happy occasion offered of presenting to you the best poem of the best poet. If I balked this opportunity, I was in despair of finding such another; and if I took it, I was still uncertain whether you would vouchsafe to accept it from my hands. It was a bold venture which I made in desiring your permission to lay my unworthy labours at your feet. But my rashness has succeeded beyond my hopes, and you have been pleased not to suffer an old man to go discontented out of the world for want of that protection of which he had been so long ambitious. I have known a gentleman in disgrace, and not daring to appear before king Charles the Second, though he much desired it; at length he took the confidence to attend a fair lady to the court, and told his majesty, that under her protection he had presumed to wait on him. With the same humble confidence I present myself before your Lordship, and attending on Virgil hope a gracious reception. The gentleman succeeded, because the powerful lady was his friend; but I have too much injured my great author to expect he should intercede for me. I would have translated him, but according to the literal

French and Italian phrases, I fear I have traduced him. It is the fault of many a well-meaning man to be officious in a wrong place, and do a prejudice where he had endeavoured to do a service. Virgil wrote his Georgics in the full strength and vigour of his age, when his judgment was at the height, and before his fancy was declining. He had (according to our homely saying) his full swing at this poem, beginning it about the age of thirty-five, and scarce concluding it before he arrived at forty. It is observed both of him and Horace, and I believe it will hold in all great poets, that though they wrote before with a certain heat of genius which inspired them, yet that heat was not perfectly digested. There is required a continuance of warmth to ripen the best and noblest fruits. Thus Horace in his first and second book of Odes was still rising, but came not to his meridian till the third. After which his judgment was an overpoise to his imagination: he grew too cautious to be bold enough; for he descended in his fourth, by flow degrees, and in his Satires and Epistles was more a philosopher and a critic than a poet. In the beginning of summer the days are almost at a stand, with little variation of length or shortness, because at that time the diurnal motion of the sun partakes more of a right line than of a spiral. The same is the method of nature in the frame of man. He seems at forty to be fully in his summer tropic; somewhat before and somewhat after he finds in his soul but small increases or decays. From fifty to threescore the balance generally holds even in our colder climates; for he loses not much in fancy, and judgment, which is the effect of observation, still increases: his succeeding years afford him little more than the stubble of his own harvest; yet, if his constitution be healthful, his mind may still retain a decent vigour; and the gleanings of that Ephraim, in comparison with others, will surpass the vintage of Abiezer. I have called this somewhere by a bold metaphor, a green old age, but Virgil has given me his authority for the figure.

DEDICATION.

Jam senior; sed cruda Deo, varidisque serectus.

Among those few who enjoy the advantage of a latter spring, your lordship is a rare example, who being now arrived at your great climacteric, yet give no proof of the least decay of your excellent judgment and comprehension of all things, which are within the compass of human understanding: Your conversation is as easy as it is instructive, and I could never observe the least vanity or the least assuming in any thing you said; but a natural unaffected modesty, full of good sense and well digested. A clearness of notion, expressed in ready and unstudied words. No man has complained, or ever can, that you have discoursed too long on any subject; for you leave us in an eagerness of learning more; pleased with what we hear, but not satisfied, because you will not speak so much as we could wish. I dare not excuse your Lordship from this fault; for though it is none in you, it is one to all who have the happiness of being known to you. I must confess the critics make it one of Virgil's beauties, that having said what he thought convenient, he always left somewhat for the imagination of his readers to supply; that they might gratify their fancies by finding more in what he had written, than at first they could, and think they had added to his thought, when it was all there before-hand, and he only saved himself the expence of words. However it was, I never went from your Lordship but with a longing to return, or without a hearty curse to him who invented ceremonies in the world, and put me on the necessity of withdrawing when it was my interest, as well as my desire, to have given you a much longer trouble. I cannot imagine (if your Lordship will give me leave to speak my thoughts) but you have had a more than ordinary vigour in your youth. For too much of heat is required at first, that there may not too little be left at last. A prodigal fire is only capable of large remains; and your's, my Lord, still burns the clearer in declining. The blaze is not so fierce as at the first, but the smoke is wholly vanished, and your friends who stand about you are not only sensible of a chearful warmth, but are kept at an awful distance by its force. In my small observations of mankind I have ever found, that such as are not rather too full of spirit when they are young, degenerate to dulness in their age. Sobriety in our riper years is the effect of a well-concocted warmth; but where the principles are only phlegm, what can be expected from the waterish matter, but an insipid manhood, and a stupid old infancy; discretion in leading-strings, and a confirmed ignorance on crutches? Virgil, in his third Georgic, when he describes a colt, who promises a courser for the race, or for the field of battle, shews him the first to pass the bridge, which trembles under him, and to stem the torrent of the flood. His beginnings must be in rashness, a noble fault; but time and experience will correct that error, and tame it into a deliberate and well-weighed courage; which knows both to be cautious and to dare, as occasion offers. Your Lordship is a man of honour, not only so unstained, but so unquestioned, that you are the living standard of that heroic virtue; so truly such, that if I would flatter you, I could not. It takes not from you, that you were born with principles of generosity and probity, but it adds to you, that you have cultivated nature, and made those principles the rule and measure of all your actions. The world knows this without my telling, yet poets have a right of recording it to all posterity.

Dignum laude virum, Musa vetat mori.

Epaminondas, Lucullus, and the two first Cæsars, were not esteemed the worse commanders, for having made philosophy and the liberal arts their study. Cicero might have been their equal, but that he wanted courage. To have both these virtues, and to have improved them both with a softness of manners, and a sweetness of conversation, few of our nobility can fill that character: one there is, and so conspicuous by his own light, that he needs not

Digito monstrari, et dicier hic est.

To be nobly born, and of an ancient family, is in the extremes of fortune either good or bad, for virtue and defcent are no inheritance. A long feries of anceftors fhews the native with great advantage at the firft ; but if he any way degenerate from his line, the leaft fpot is vifible on ermine. But to preferve this whitenefs in its original purity, you, my Lord, have, like that ermine, forfaken the common track of bufinefs, which is not always clean: you have chofen for yourfelf a private greatnefs, and will not be polluted with ambition. It has been obferved in former times, that none have been fo greedy of employments, and of managing the public, as they who have leaft deferved their ftations. But fuch only merit to be called patriots, under whom we fee their country flourifh. I have laughed fometimes (for who would always be a Heraclitus ?) when I have reflected on thofe men, who from time to time have fhot themfelves into the world. I have feen many fucceffions of them, fome bolting out upon the ftage with vaft applaufe, and others hiffed off, and quitting it with difgrace. But while they were in action I have constantly obferved, that they feemed defirous to retreat from bufinefs: greatnefs they faid was naufeous, and a crowd was troublefome; a quiet privacy was their ambition. Some few of them I believe faid this in earneft, and were making a provifion againft future want, that they might enjoy their age with eafe: they faw the happinefs of a private life, and promifed to themfelves a bleffing, which every day it was in their power to poffefs. But they deferred it, and lingered ftill at court, becaufe they thought they had not yet enough to make them happy; they would have more, and laid in to make their folitude luxurious. A wretched philofophy, which Epicurus never taught them in his garden: they loved the profpect of this quiet in reverfion, but were not willing to have it in poffeffion; they would firft be old, and made as fure of health and life, as if both of them were at their difpofe. But put them to the neceffity of a prefent choice, and they preferred continuance in power: like the wretch who called death to his affiftance, but re-

DEDICATION.

fused him when he came. The great Scipio was not of their opinion, who indeed sought honours in his youth, and indured the fatigues with which he purchased them. He served his country when it was in need of his courage and conduct, until he thought it was time to serve himself; but dismounted from the saddle when he found the beast which bore him began to grow restiff and ungovernable. But your Lordship has given us a better example of moderation. You saw betimes that ingratitude is not confined to commonwealths; and therefore though you were formed alike, for the greatest of civil employments and military commands, yet you pushed not your fortune to rise in either, but contented yourself with being capable, as much as any whosoever, of defending your country with your sword, or assisting it with your counsel, when you were called. For the rest the respect and love which was paid you, not only in the province where you live, but generally by all who had the happiness to know you, was a wise exchange for the honours, of the court: a place of forgetfulness, at the best, for well-deservers. It is necessary for the polishing of manners to have breathed that air, but it is infectious even to the best morals to live always in it. It is a dangerous commerce where an honest man is sure at the first of being cheated; and he recovers not his losses, but by learning to cheat others. The undermining smile becomes at length habitual; and the drift of his plausible conversation is only to flatter one, that he may betray another. Yet it is good to have been a looker-on, without venturing to play; that a man may know false dice another time, though he never means to use them. I commend not him who never knew a court, but him who forsakes it because he knows it. A young man deserves no praise, who out of melancholy zeal leaves the world before he has well tried it, and runs headlong into religion. He who carries a maidenhead into a cloister, is sometimes apt to lose it there, and to repent of his repentance. He only is like to endure austerities, who has already found the inconvenience of pleasures. For almost every man will be making experiments in one part or another of his life: and the danger is the less when we are young; for having tried it early, we shall not be apt to repeat it afterwards. Your Lordship therefore may properly be said to have chosen a retreat, and not to have chosen it until you had maturely weighed the advantages of rising higher with the hazards of the fall. " Res non parta labore, sed relicta," was thought by a poet to be one of the requisites to a happy life. Why should a reasonable man put it into the power of fortune to make him miserable, when his ancestors have taken care to release him from her? let him venture, says Horace, " Qui zonam perdidit." He who has nothing, plays securely, for he may win, and cannot be poorer if he loses. But he who is born to a plentiful estate, and is ambitious of offices at court, sets a stake to fortune, which she can seldom answer: if he gains nothing, he loses all, or part of what was once his own; and if he gets, he cannot be certain but he may refund.

DEDICATION.

In short, however he succeeds, it is covetousness that induced him first to play, and covetousness is the undoubted sign of ill sense at bottom. The odds are against him, that he loses; and one loss may be of more consequence to him than all his former winnings. It is like the present war of the Christians against the Turk; every year they gain a victory, and by that a town; but if they are once defeated they lose a province at a blow, and endanger the safety of the whole empire. You, my Lord, enjoy your quiet in a garden, where you have not only the leisure of thinking, but the pleasure to think of nothing which can discompose your mind. A good conscience is a port which is land-locked on every side, and where no winds can possibly invade, no tempests can arise. There a man may stand upon the shore, and not only see his own image, but that of his Maker, clearly reflected from the undisturbed and silent waters. Reason was intended for a blessing, and such it is to men of honour and integrity; who desire no more than what they are able to give themselves; like the happy old Coricyan, whom my author describes in his fourth Georgic; whose fruits and sallads, on which he lived contented, were all of his own growth, and his own plantation. Virgil seems to think that the blessings of a country life are not complete without an improvement of knowledge by contemplation and reading.

> O fortunatos nimiùm, bona si sua norint,
> Agricolas!

It is but half possession not to understand that happiness which we possess: a foundation of good sense, and a cultivation of learning, are required to give a seasoning to retirement, and make us taste the blessing. God has bestowed on your Lordship the first of these, and you have bestowed on yourself the second. Eden was not made for beasts, though they were suffered to live in it, but for their master, who studied God in the works of his creation. Neither could the devil have been happy there with all his knowledge, for he wanted innocence to make him so. He brought envy, malice and ambition into paradise, which soured

DEDICATION.

to him the sweetness of the place. Wherever inordinate affections are, it is hell. Such only can enjoy the country, who are capable of thinking when they are there, and have left their passions behind them in the town. Then they are prepared for solitude; and in that solitude is prepared for them

Et secura quies, et nescia fallere vita.

As I began this dedication with a verse of Virgil, so I conclude it with another. The continuance of your health, to enjoy that happiness which you so well deserve, and which you have provided for yourself, is the sincere and earnest wish of

Your Lordship's

most devoted and

most obedient servant,

JOHN DRYDEN.

AN ESSAY ON THE GEORGICS,

By Mr. ADDISON.

VIRGIL may be reckoned the first who introduced three new kinds of Poetry among the Romans, which he copied after three the greatest masters of Greece. Theocritus and Homer have still disputed for the advantage over him in pastoral and heroics, but I think all are unanimous in giving him the precedence to Hesiod in his Georgics. The truth of it is, the sweetness and rusticity of a pastoral cannot be so well exprest in any other tongue as in the Greek, when rightly mixed and qualified with the Doric dialect, nor can the majesty of an heroic poem any where appear so well as in this language, which has a natural greatness in it, and can be often rendered more deep and sonorous by the pronunciation of the Ionians. But in the middle stile, where the writers in both tongues are on a level, we see how far Virgil has excelled all who have written in the same way with him.

There has been abundance of criticism spent on Virgil's Pastorals and Æneids, but the Georgics are a subject which none of the critics have sufficiently taken into their consideration; most of them passing it over in silence, or casting it under the same head with Pastoral; a division by no means proper, unless we suppose the stile of a husbandman ought to be imitated in a Georgic, as that of a shepherd is in Pastoral. But though the scene of both these poems lies in the same place, the speakers in them are of a quite different character, since the precepts of husbandry are not to be delivered with the simplicity of a plough-man, but with the address of a poet. No rules therefore that relate to Pastoral, can any way affect the Georgics, which fall under that class of poetry, which consists in giving plain and direct instructions to the reader; whether they be moral duties, as those of Theognis and Pythagoras; or philosophical speculations, as those of Aratus and Lucretius; or rules of practice, as those of Hesiod and Virgil. Among these different kinds of subjects, that which the Georgics goes upon, is I think the meanest and least improving, but the most pleasing and delightful. Precepts of morality, besides the natural corruption of our tempers, which makes us averse to them, are so abstracted from ideas of sense, that they seldom give an opportunity for those beautiful descriptions and images which are the spirit and life of poetry. Natural philosophy has indeed sensible objects to work upon, but then it often puzzles the reader with the intricacy of its notions and perplexes him with a multitude of its disputes. But this kind of poetry I am now speaking of, addresses itself wholly to the imagination;

it is altogether conversant among the fields and woods, and has the most delightful part of nature for its province. It raises in our minds a pleasing variety of scenes and landscapes, whilst it teaches us; and makes the driest of its precepts look like a description. "A Georgic therefore is some part of the science of husbandry put into a pleasing dress, and set off with all the beauties and embellishments of poetry. Now since this science of husbandry is of a very large extent, the poet shews his skill in singling out such precepts to proceed on, as are useful, and at the same time most capable of ornament. Virgil was so well acquainted with this secret, that to set off his first Georgic, he has run into a set of precepts, which are almost foreign to his subject, in that beautiful account he gives us of the signs in nature, which precede the changes of the weather.

And if there be so much art in the choice of fit precepts, there is so much more required in the treating of them; that they may fall in after each other by a natural unforced method, and shew themselves in the best and most advantageous light. They should all be so finely wrought together in the same piece, that no coarse seam may discover where they join, as in a curious brede of needlework, one colour falls away by such just degrees, and another rises so insensibly, that we see the variety without being able to distinguish the total vanishing of the one from the first appearance of the other. Nor is it sufficient to range and dispose this body of precepts into a clear and easy method, unless they are delivered to us in the most pleasing and agreeable manner: for there are several ways of conveying the same truth to the mind of man; and to choose the pleasantest of these ways, is that which chiefly distinguishes poetry from prose, and makes Virgil's rules of husbandry pleasanter to read than Varro's. Where the prose-writer tells us plainly what ought to be done, the poet often conceals the precept in a description, and represents his countryman performing the action in which he would instruct his reader. Where the one sets out as fully and distinctly as he can, all the parts of the truth, which he would communicate to us; the other singles out the most pleasing circumstance of this truth, and so conveys the whole in a more diverting manner to the understanding. I shall give one instance out of a multitude of this nature that might be found in the Georgics, where the reader may see the different ways Virgil has taken to express the same thing, and how much pleasanter every manner of expression is, than the plain and direct mention of it would have been. It is in the second Georgic, where he tells us what trees will bear grafting on each other.

> Et sæpe alterius ramos impune videmus
> Vertere in alterius, mutatamque insita mala
> Ferre pyrum, et prunis lapidosa rubescere corna.
> ——Steriles Platani malos gessere valentes,
> Castaneæ fagos, ornusque incanuit albo
> Flore pyri: glandemque suis fregere sub ulmis.
> ——Nec longum tempus: et ingens
> Exiit ad cœlum ramis felicibus arbos:
> Miraturque novas frondes et non sua poma.

Here we see the poet considered all the effects of this union between trees of different kinds, and took notice of that effect which had the most surprize, and by consequence the most delight in it, to express the capacity that was in them of being thus united. This way of writing is every where much in use among the poets, and is particularly practised by Virgil, who loves to suggest a truth indirectly, and without giving us a full and open view of it; to let us see just so much as will naturally lead the imagination into all the parts that lie concealed. This is wonderfully diverting to the understanding, thus to receive a precept, that enters as it were through a bye-way, and to apprehend an idea that draws a whole train after it. For here the mind, which is always delighted with its own discoveries, only takes the hint from the poet, and seems to work out the rest by the strength of her own faculties.

But since the inculcating precept upon precept, will at length prove tiresome to the reader, if he meets with no entertainment, the poet must take care not to encumber his poem with too much business; but sometimes to relieve the subject with a moral reflection, or let it rest a while, for the sake of a pleasant and pertinent digression. Nor is it sufficient to run out into beautiful and diverting digressions (as it is generally thought) unless they are brought in aptly, and are something of a piece with the main design of the Georgic: for they ought to have a remote alliance at least to the subject, that so the whole poem may be more uniform and agreeable in all its parts. We should never quite lose sight of the country, though we are sometimes entertained with a distant prospect of it. Of this nature are Virgil's descriptions of the original of agriculture, of the fruitfulness of Italy, of a country life, and the like, which are not brought in by force, but naturally rise out of the principal argument and design of the poem. I know no one digression in the Georgics that may seem to contradict this observation, besides that in the latter end of the first book, where the poet launches out into a discourse of the battle of Pharsalia, and the actions of Augustus: but it is worth while to consider how admirably he has turned the course of his narration into its proper channel, and made his husbandman concerned even in what relates to the battle, in those inimitable lines.

> Scilicet et tempus veniet, cum finibus illis
> Agricola incurvo terram molitus aratro,
> Exesa inveniet scabra rubigine pila:
> Aut gravibus rastris galeas pulsabit inanes,
> Grandiaque effossis mirabitur ossa sepulchris.

And afterwards speaking of Augustus's actions, he still remembers that agriculture ought to be some way hinted at throughout the whole poem,

> ———Non ullus aratro
> Dignus honos: squalent abductis arva colonis:
> Et curvæ rigidum falces conflantur in ensem.

We now come to the stile which is proper to a Georgic: and indeed this is the part on which the poet must lay out all his strength, that his words may be warm and glowing, and that every thing he describes may immediately present itself, and rise up to the reader's view. He ought in particular to be careful of not letting his subject debase his stile, and betray him into a meanness of expression, but every where to keep up his verse in all the pomp of numbers and dignity of words.

I think nothing which is a phrase or saying in common talk, should be admitted into a serious poem; because it takes off from the solemnity of the expression, and gives it too great a turn of familiarity: much less ought the low phrases and terms of art, that are adapted to husbandry, have any place in such a work as the Georgic, which is not to appear in the natural simplicity and nakedness of its subject, but in the pleasantest dress that poetry can bestow on it. Thus Virgil, to deviate from the common form of words, would not make use of "tempore" but "sy-

"dere" in his first verse, and every where else abounds with metaphors, Grecisms, and circumlocutions, to give his verse the greater pomp, and preserve it from sinking into a plebeian stile. And herein consists Virgil's masterpiece, who has not only excelled all other poets, but even himself, in the language of his Georgics, where we receive more strong and lively ideas of things from his words, than we could have done from the objects themselves; and find our imaginations more affected by his descriptions, than they would have been by the very sight of what he describes.

I shall now, after this short scheme of rules, consider the different success that Hesiod and Virgil have met with in this kind of poetry, which may give us some further notion of the excellence of the Georgics. To begin with Hesiod; if we may guess at his character from his writings, he had much more of the husbandman than the poet in his temper; he was wonderfully grave, discreet, and frugal; he lived altogether in the country, and was, probably for his great prudence, the oracle of the whole neighbourhood. These principles of good husbandry ran through his works, and directed him to the choice of tillage and merchandize, for the subject of that which is the most celebrated of them. He is every where bent on instruction, avoids all manner of digressions, and does not stir out of the field once in the whole Georgic. His method in describing month after month with its proper seasons and employments, is too grave and simple; it takes off from the surprize and variety of the poem, and makes the whole look but like a modern almanack in verse. The reader is carried through a course of weather, and may beforehand guess whether he is to meet with snow or rain, clouds or sunshine, in the next description. His descriptions indeed have abundance of nature in them, but then it is nature in her simplicity and undress. Thus when he speaks of January, "The wild beasts," says he, "run shi-vering through the woods with their heads stooping to the ground, and their tails clapt between their legs; the goats and oxen are almost flead with cold; but it is not so bad with the sheep, because they have a thick coat of wool about them. The old men too are bitterly pinched with the weather, but the young girls feel nothing of it, who sit at home with their mothers by a warm fire-side." Thus does the old gentleman give himself up to a loose kind of tattle, rather than endeavour after a just poetical description. Nor has he shewn more of art or judgment in the precepts he has given us, which are sown so very thick, that they clog the poem too much, and are often so minute and full of circumstances, that they weaken and un-nerve his verse. But after all, we are beholden to him for the first rough sketch of a Georgic: where we may still discover something venerable in the antiqueness of the work; but if we would see the design enlarged, the figures reformed, the colouring laid on, and the whole piece finished, we must expect it from a greater master's hands.

Virgil has drawn out the rules of tillage and planting into two books, which Hesiod has dispatched in half a one: but has so raised the natural rudeness and simplicity of his subject with such a significancy of expression, such a pomp of verse, such variety of transitions, and such a solemn air in his reflections, that if we look on both poets together, we see in one the plainness of a downright countryman, and in the other, something of a rustic majesty, like that of a Roman dictator at the plough-tail. He delivers the meanest of his precepts with a kind of grandeur, he breaks the clods and tosses the dung about with an air of gracefulness. His prognostications of the weather are taken out of Aratus, where we may see how judiciously he has picked out those that are most proper for his husbandman's observation; how he has enforced the expression, and heightened the images which he found in the original.

The second book has more wit in it, and a greater boldness in its metaphors than any of the rest. The poet with a great beauty applies oblivion, ignorance, wonder, desire, and the like, to his trees. The last Georgic has indeed as many metaphors, but not so daring as this; for human thoughts and passions may be more naturally ascribed to a bee, than to an inanimate plant. He who reads over the pleasures of a country life, as they are described by Virgil in the latter end of this book, can scarce be of Virgil's mind in preferring even the life of a philosopher to it.

We may, I think, read the poet's clime in his description, for he seems to have been in a sweat at the writing of it.

———O quis me gelidis sub montibus Hæmi
Sistat, et ingenti ramorum protegat umbra?

And is every where mentioning among his chief pleasures, the coolness of his shades and rivers, vales and grottos, which a more northern poet would have omitted for the description of a sunny hill and fire-side.

The third Georgic seems to be the most laboured of them all; there is a wonderful vigour and spirit in the description of the horse and chariot-race. The force of love is represented in noble instances, and very sublime expressions. The Scythian winter-piece appears so very cold and bleak to the eye, that a man can scarce look on it without shivering. The murrain at the end has all the expressiveness that words can give. It was here that the poet strained hard to out-do Lucretius in the description of his plague; and if the reader would see what success he had, he may find it at large in Scaliger.

But Virgil seems no where so well pleased as when he is got among his bees in the fourth Georgic; and ennobles the actions of so trivial a creature, with metaphors drawn from the most important concerns of mankind. His verses are not in a greater noise and hurry in the battles of Æneas and Turnus, than in the engagement of two swarms. And as in his Æneis he compares the labour of his Trojans to those of bees and pismires, here he compares the labours of the bees to those of the Cyclops. In short, the last Georgic was a good prelude to the Æneis; and very well shewed what the poet could do in the description of what was really great, by his describing the mock-grandeur of an insect with so good a grace. There is more pleasantness in the little platform of a garden, which he gives us about the middle of this book, than in all the spacious walks and water-works of Rapin. The speech of Proteus, at the end, can never be enough admired, and was indeed very fit to conclude so divine a work.

After this particular account of the beauties in the Georgics, I should in the next place endeavour to point out it's imperfections, if it has any. But though I think there are some few parts in it that are not so beautiful as the rest, I shall not presume to name them, as rather suspecting my own judgment, than I can believe a fault to be in that poem, which lay so long under Virgil's correction, and had his last hand put to it. The first Georgic was probably burlesqued in the author's lifetime; for we still find in the scholiasts a verse that ridicules part of a line translated from Hesiod; "nudus ara, sere nudus."—— And we may easily guess at the judgment of this extraordinary critic, whoever he was, from his censuring this particular precept. We may be sure Virgil would not have translated it from Hesiod, had he not discovered some beauty in it; and indeed the beauty of it is what I before observed to be frequently met with in Virgil, the delivering the precept so indirectly, and singling out the particular circumstances of sowing and ploughing naked, to suggest to us that these employments are proper only in the hot season of the year.

I shall not here compare the stile of the Georgics with that of Lucretius, which the reader may see already done in the Preface to the second volume of Miscellany Poems; but shall conclude this poem to be the most complete, elaborate, and finished piece of all antiquity. The Æneis indeed is of a nobler kind, but the Georgic is more perfect in its kind. The Æneis has a greater variety of beauties in it, but those of the Georgic are more exquisite. In short, the Georgic has all the perfections that can be expected in a poem written by the greatest poet in the flower of his age, when his invention was ready, his imagination warm, his judgment settled, and all his faculties in their full vigour and maturity.

VIRGIL's
GEORGIGS.

GEORGIC I.

THE ARGUMENT.

The poet, in the beginning of this book, propounds the general design of each Georgic: and, after a solemn invocation of all the Gods who are any way related to his subject, he addresses himself in particular to Augustus, whom he compliments with divinity; and after strikes into his business. He shews the different kinds of tillage proper to different soils, traces out the original of agriculture, gives a catalogue of the husbandman's tools, specifies the employments peculiar to each season, describes the changes of the weather, with the signs in heaven and earth that forebode them. Instances many of the prodigies that happened near the time of Julius Cæsar's death. And shuts up all with a supplication to the Gods for the safety of Augustus, and the preservation of Rome.

THE FIRST BOOK OF THE GEORGICS.

WHAT makes a plenteous harvest, when to turn
The fruitful soil, and when to sow the corn;
The care of sheep, of oxen, and of kine,
And how to raise on elms the teeming vine;
The birth and genius of the frugal bee,   5
I sing, Mecænas, and I sing to thee.

   Ye Deities! who fields and plains protect,
Who rule the seasons, and the year direct;
Bacchus and fost'ring Ceres, Pow'rs divine,
Who gave us corn for mast, for water wine: 10

Ye Fauns, propitious to the rural swains,
Ye Nymphs that haunt the mountains and the plains,
Join in my work, and to my numbers bring
Your needful succour, for your gifts I sing.
And thou, whose trident struck the teeming earth,
And made a passage for the courser's birth; 16
And thou, for whom the Cæan shore sustains
The milky herds that graze the flow'ry plains;
And thou, the shepherd's tutelary God,
Leave, for a while, O Pan! thy lov'd abode; 20
And, if Arcadian fleeces be thy care,
From fields and mountains to my song repair.
Inventor, Pallas, of the fatt'ning oil,
Thou founder of the plough and ploughman's toil;
And thou, whose hands the shroud-like cypress
    rear; 25
Come all ye Gods and Goddesses that wear
The rural honours, and increase the year.
You, who supply the ground with seeds of grain;
And you, who swell those seeds with kindly rain:
And chiefly thou, whose undetermin'd state 30
Is yet the business of the Gods debate;
Whether in after-times to be declared
The patron of the world, and Rome's peculiar
    guard,

Or o'er the fruits and seasons to preside,
And the round circuit of the year to guide; 35
Pow'rful of blessings, which thou strew'st around,
And with thy Goddess mother's myrtle crown'd.
Or wilt thou, Cæsar, chuse the wat'ry reign,
To smooth the surges, and correct the main?
Then mariners, in storms, to thee shall pray, 40
Ev'n utmost Thulè shall thy pow'r obey;
And Neptune shall resign the fasces of the sea.
The wat'ry virgins for thy bed shall strive,
And Tethys all her waves in dowry give.
Or wilt thou bless our summers with thy rays, 45
And seated near the Balance, poise the days:
Where in the void of heav'n a space is free,
Betwixt the Scorpion and the Maid, for thee.
The Scorpion ready to receive thy laws,
Yields half his region, and contracts his claws. 50
Whatever part of heav'n thou shalt obtain,
For let not hell presume of such a reign;
Nor let so dire a thirst of empire move
Thy mind, to leave thy kindred Gods above.
Tho' Greece admires Elisium's blest retreat, 55
Tho' Proserpine affects her silent seat,
And, importun'd by Ceres to remove,
Prefers the fields below to those above.

But thou, propitious Cæsar! guide my course,
And to my bold endeavours add thy force. 60
Pity the poet's and the ploughman's cares,
Int'rest thy greatness in our mean affairs,
And use thyself betimes to hear and grant our
　　pray'rs.
　While yet the spring is young, while earth un-
　　binds
Her frozen bosom to the western winds; 65
While mountain-snows dissolve against the sun,
And streams yet new, from precipices run;
Ev'n in this early dawning of the year,
Produce the plough, and yoke the sturdy steer.
And goad him till ye groans beneath his toil, 70
Till the bright share is bury'd in the soil.
That crop rewards the greedy peasant's pains,
Which twice the sun, and twice the cold sustains,
And bursts the crowded barns, with more than
　　promis'd gains.
But ere we stir the yet unbroken ground, 75
The various course of seasons must be found;
The weather, and the setting of the winds,
The culture suiting to the sev'ral kinds
Of seeds and plants, and what will thrive and rise,
And what the genius of the soil denies. 80

This ground with Bacchus, that with Ceres suits:
That other loads the trees with happy fruits;
A fourth with grass, unbidden, decks the ground:
Thus Tmolus is with yellow saffron crown'd;
India, black ebon and white ivory bears; 85
And soft Idume weeps her od'rous tears.
Thus Pontus sends her beaver stones from far,
And naked Spaniards temper steel for war.
Epirus for th' Elean chariot breeds
(In hopes of palms) a race of running steeds. 90
This is th' original contract; these the laws
Impos'd by nature, and by nature's cause,
On sundry places, when Deucalion hurl'd
His mother's entrails on the desart world:
Whence men, a hard laborious kind were born.
Then borrow part of winter for thy corn; 96
And early with thy team the glebe in furrows turn.
That while the turf lies open and unbound,
Succeeding suns may bake the mellow ground.
But if the soil be barren, only fear 100
The surface, and but lightly print the share,
When cold Arcturus rises with the sun;
Lest wicked weeds the corn should over-run.

In wat'ry foils: or left the barren sand
Should fuck the moisture from the thirsty land. 105
Both these unhappy foils the swain forbears,
And keeps a sabbath of alternate years;
That the spent earth may gather heat again,
And, better'd by cessation, bear the grain.
At least where vetches, pulse, and tares have stood,
And stalks of lupines grew (a stubborn wood.) 110
Th' ensuing season, in return, may bear
The bearded product of the golden year.
For flax and oats will burn the tender field,
And sleeppy poppies harmful harvests yield. 115
But sweet vicissitudes of rest and toil
Make easy labour, and renew the soil.
Yet sprinkle sordid ashes all around,
And load with fatt'ning dung thy fallow ground.
Thus change of seeds for meagre soils is best; 120
And earth manur'd, not idle, though at rest.

 Long practice has a sure improvement found,
With kindled fires to burn the barren ground,
When the light stubble, to the flames resign'd
Is driv'n along, and crackles in the wind. 125
Whether from hence the hollow womb of earth
Is warm'd with secret strength for better birth;

Or when the latent vice is cur'd by fire,
Redundant humours thro' the pores expire;   129
Or that the warmth diftends the chinks, and makes
New breathings, whence new nourifhment fhe
    takes;
Or that the heat the gaping ground conftrains,
New knits the furface, and new ftrings the veins,
Left foaking fhow'rs fhould pierce her fecret feat,
Or freezing Boreas chill her genial heat;   135
Or fcorching funs too violently beat.

   Nor is the profit fmall, the peafant makes,
Who fmooths with harrows, or who pounds with
    rakes,
The crumbling clods: nor Ceres from on high
Regards his labours with a grudging eye;   140
Nor his, who plows acrofs the furrow'd grounds,
And on the back of earth inflicts new wounds;
For he with frequent exercife commands
Th'-unwilling foil, and tames the ftubborn lands.

   Ye fwains, invoke the Pow'rs who rule the fky,
For a moift fummer, and a winter dry: 145
For winter drought rewards the peafant's pain,
And broods indulgent on the bury'd grain.

Hence Mysia boasts her harvests, and the tops
Of Gargarus admire their happy crops.   150
When first the soil receives the fruitful seed,
Make no delay, but cover it with speed:
So fenc'd from cold; the pliant furrows break,
Before the surly clod resists the rake.
And call the floods from high, to rush amain   155
With pregnant streams, to swell the teeming
    grain.
Then when the fiery suns too fiercely play,
And shrivell'd herbs on with'ring stems decay,
The wary ploughman, on the mountain's brow,
Undams his wat'ry stores, huge torrents flow;   160
And, rattling down the rocks, large moisture yield,
Temp'ring the thirsty fever of the field.
And lest the stem, too feeble for the freight,
Shou'd scarce sustain the head's unwieldy weight,
Sends in his feeding flocks betimes t' invade   165
The rising bulk of the luxuriant blade;
Ere yet th' aspiring offspring of the grain
O'ertops the ridges of the furrow'd plain:
And drains the standing waters, when they yield
Too large a bev'rage to the drunken field.   170

But most in autumn, and the show'ry spring,
When dubious months uncertain weather bring;
When fountains open, when impetuous rain
Swells hasty brooks, and pours upon the plain;
When earth with slime and mud is cover'd o'er,   175
Or hollow places spue their wat'ry store.
Nor yet the ploughman, nor the lab'ring steer,
Sustain alone the hazards of the year;
But glutton geese, and the Strymonian crane,
With foreign troops invade the tender grain: 180
And tow'ring weeds malignant shadows yield;
And spreading succ'ry chokes the rising field.
The sire of Gods and men, with hard decrees,
Forbids our plenty to be bought with ease:
And wills that mortal men, inur'd to toil,   185
Shou'd exercise, with pain, the grudging soil.
Himself invented first the shining share,
And whetted human industry by care:
Himself did handy-crafts and arts ordain;
Nor suffer'd sloth to rust his active reign.   190
Ere this, no peasant vex'd the peaceful ground,
Which only turfs and greens for altars found:
No fences parted fields, nor marks nor bounds
Distinguish'd acres of litigious grounds:

But all was common, and the fruitful earth 195
Was free to give her unexacted birth.
Jove added venom to the viper's brood,
And swell'd with raging storms, the peaceful flood:
Commission'd hungry wolves t' infest the fold,
And shook from oaken leaves the liquid gold. 200
Remov'd from human reach the chearful fire,
And from the rivers bade the wine retire:
That studious need might useful arts explore,
From furrow'd fields to reap the foodful store;
And force the veins of clashing flints t' expire 205
The lurking seeds of their celestial fire.
Then first on seas the hollow'd alder swam;
Then sailors quarter'd heav'n, and found a name
For ev'ry fix'd and every wand'ring star:
The Pleiads, Hyads, and the Northern Car. 210
Then toils for beasts, and lime for birds were found,
And deep-mouth'd dogs did forest walks surround:
And casting nets were spread in shallow brooks,
Drags in the deep, and baits were hung on hooks.
Then saws were tooth'd, and sounding axes made;
(For wedges first did yielding wood invade,) 216
And various arts in order did succeed.
(What cannot endless labour, urg'd by need?)

First Ceres taught, the ground with grain to sow,
And arm'd with iron shares the crooked plough; 220
When now Dodonian oaks no more supply'd
Their mast, and trees their forest fruit deny'd.
Soon was his labour doubled to the swain,
And blasting mildews blacken'd all his grain.
Tough thistles chok'd the fields, and kill'd the corn,
And an unthrifty crop of weeds was borne. 226
Then burrs and brambles, an unbidden crew
Of graceless guests, th' unhappy field subdue:
And oats unbless'd, and darnel domineers,
And shoots its head above the shining ears. 230
So that unless the land with daily care
Is exercis'd, and with an iron war
Or rakes and harrows, the proud foes expell'd,
And birds with clamours frighted from the field;
Unless the boughs are lopp'd that shade the plain,
And heav'n invok'd with vows for fruitful rain, 236
On other crops you may with envy look,
And shake for food the long-abandon'd oak.
Nor must we pass untold what arms they wield,
Who labour tillage and the furrow'd field: 240
Without whose aid the ground her corn denies,
And nothing can be sown, and nothing rise.

The crooked plough, the share, the tow'ring height
Of waggons, and the cart's unweildly weight;
The shed, the tumbril, hurdles, and the flail,   245
The fan of Bacchus, with the flying sail.
These all must be prepar'd, if ploughmen hope
The promis'd blessing of a bounteous crop.
Young elms with early force in copses bow,
Fit for the figure of the crooked plough.   250
Of eight feet long a fast'ned beam prepare,
On either side the head produce an ear,
And sink a socket for the shining share.
Of beech the plough-tail, and the bending yoke;
Or softer linden harden'd in the smoke,   255
I cou'd be long in precepts, but I fear
So mean a subject might offend your ear.
Delve of convenient depth your threshing floor;
With temper'd clay then fill and face it o'er:
And let the weighty roller run the round,   260
To smooth the surface of th' unequal ground;
Lest crack'd with summer heats the flooring flies,
Or sinks, and thro' the crannies weeds arise.
For sundry foes the rural realms surround;
The field-mouse builds her garner under ground.

For gather'd grain the blind laborious mole 266
In winding mazes works her hidden hole.
In hollow caverns vermin make abode,
The hissing serpent, and the swelling toad:
The corn-devouring weazel here abides, 270
And the wise ant her wintry store provides.

    Mark well the flow'ring almonds in the wood;
If od'rous blooms the bearing branches load,
The glebe will answer to the sylvan reign,
Great heats will follow, and large crops of grain.
But if a wood of leaves o'ershade the tree, 276
Such and so barren will thy harvest be:
In vain the hind shall vex the threshing-floor,
For empty chaff and straw will be thy store.
Some steep their seed, and some in cauldrons boil
With vigorous nitre, and with lees of oil, 281
O'er gentle fires; th' exuberant juice to drain,
And swell the flatt'ring husks with fruitful grain.
Yet is not the success for years assur'd,
Tho' chosen is the seed, and fully cured; 285
Unless the peasant, with his annual pain,
Renews his choice, and culls the largest grain.
Thus all below, whether by Nature's curse,
Or Fate's decree, degen'rate still to worse.

So the boat's brawny crew the current stem,   290
And, flow advancing, struggle with the stream:
But if they flack their hands, or cease to strive,
Then down the flood with headlong haste they
  drive.

Nor must the ploughman less observe the skies,
When the Kids, Dragon, and Arcturus rise,   295
Then sailors homeward bent, who cut their way
Thro' Helle's stormy straits, and oister-breeding sea.
But when Astrea's balance hung on high,
Betwixt the nights and days divides the sky,
Then yoke your oxen, sow your winter grain;   300
Till cold December comes with driving rain.
Linseed and fruitful poppy bury warm,
In a dry season, and prevent the storm.
Sow beans and clover in a rotten soil,
And millet, rising from your annual toil.   305
When with his golden horns, in full career,
The Bull beats down the barriers of the year;
And Argos and the Dog forsake the northern
  sphere.

But if your care to wheat alone extend,
Let Maia with her sisters first descend,   310
And the bright Gnosian diadem downward bend,

Before you truſt in earth your future hope;
Or elſe expect a liſtleſs lazy crop.
Some ſwains have ſown before, but moſt have found
A huſky harveſt from the grudging ground.   315
Vile vetches would you ſow, or lentils lean,
The growth of Egypt, or the kidney-bean!
Begin when the ſlow Waggoner deſcends;
Nor ceaſe your ſowing till mid-winter ends:
For this, thro' twelve bright ſigns Apollo guides   320
The year, and earth in ſev'ral climes divides.
Five girdles binds the ſkies, the torrid zone
Glows with the paſſing and repaſſing ſun.
Far on the right and left, th' extremes of heav'n,
To froſts and ſnows the bitter blaſts are given.   325
Betwixt the midſt and theſe, the Gods aſſign'd
Two habitable ſeats for human kind:
And croſs their limits cut a ſloping way,
Which the twelve ſigns in beauteous order ſway,
Two poles turn round the globe; one ſeen to riſe
O'er Scythian hills, and one in Lybian ſkies.   331
The firſt ſublime in heav'n, the laſt is whirl'd
Below the regions of the nether world.
Around our pole the ſpiry Dragon glides,
And like a winding ſtream the Bears divides;   335

The Less and Greater, who by Fate's decree
Abhor to dive beneath the southern sea;
There, as they say, perpetual night is found
In silence brooding on th' unhappy ground:
Or when Aurora leaves our northern sphere, 340
She lights the downward heav'n, and rises there.
And when on us she breathes the living light,
Red vesper kindles there the tapers of the night.
From hence uncertain seasons we may know,
And when to reap the grain, and when to sow;
Or when to fell the furzes; when 'tis meet 345
To spread the flying canvas for the fleet.
Observe what stars arise or disappear;
And the four quarters of the rolling year.
But when cold weather and continued rain, 350
The lab'ring husband in his house restrain,
Let him forecast his work with timely care,
Which else is huddled when the skies are fair:
Then let him mark the sheep, or whet the shining
 share,
Or hollow trees for boats, or number o'er 355
His sacks, or measure his increasing store;
Or sharpen stakes, or head the forks, or twine
The sallow twigs to tie the straggling vine;

Or wicker baskets weave, or air the corn,
Or grinded grain betwixt two marbles turn.   360
No laws, divine or human, can restrain
From necessary works the lab'ring swain.
Ev'n holy-days and feasts permission yield,
To float the meadows, or to fence the field;
To fire the brambles, snare the birds, and steep   365
In wholsome water-falls the woolly sheep.
And oft the drudging ass is driv'n, with toil,
To neighb'ring towns with apples and with oil:
Returning late, and loaden home with gain
Of barter'd pitch, and hand-mills for the grain.

The lucky days in each revolving moon,
For labour chuse: the fifth be sure to shun;   370
That gave the Furies and pale Pluto birth,
And arm'd against the skies, the sons of earth.
With mountains pil'd on mountains, thrice they strove   375
To scale the steepy battlements of Jove;
And thrice his lightning and red thunder play'd,
And their demolish'd works in ruin laid.
The sev'nth is, next the tenth, the best to join
Young oxen to the yoke, and plant the vine.   380

Then weavers stretch your stays upon the weft:
The ninth is good for travel, bad for theft.
Some works in dead of night are better done:
Or when the morning dew prevents the sun.
Parch'd meads and stubble mow, by Phœbe's light,
Which both require the coolness of the night: 386
For moisture then abounds, and pearly rains
Descend in silence to refresh the plains.
The wife and husband equally conspire,
To work by night, and rake the winter fire: 390
He sharpens torches in the glimm'ring room,
She shoots the flying shuttle through the loom;
Or boils in kettles musts of wine, and skims
With leaves, the dregs that overflow the brims.
And till the watchful cock awakes the day, 395
She sings to drive the tedious hours away.
But in warm weather, when the skies are clear,
By day-light reap the product of the year;
And in the sun your golden grain display,
And thresh it out, and winnow it by day. 400
Plough naked, swain, and naked sow the land,
For lazy winter numbs the lab'ring hand.
In genial winter, swains enjoy their store,
Forget their hardships, and recruit for more.

The farmer to full bowls invites his friends, 405
And what he got with pains, with pleasure spends.
So sailors, when escap'd from stormy seas,
First crown their vessels, then indulge their ease.
Yet that's the proper time to thresh the wood
For mast of oak, your father's homely food. 410
To gather laurel-berries, and the spoil
Of bloody myrtles, and to press your oil.
For stalking canes to set the guileful snare,
T' inclose the stags in toils, and hunt the hare.
With Balearic slings, or Gnosian bow, 415
To persecute from far the flying doe.
Then, when the fleecy skies new clothe the wood,
And cakes of rustling ice come rolling down the
    flood.

  Now sing we stormy stars, when autumn weighs
The year, and adds to nights, and shortens
    days; 420
And suns declining shine with feeble rays:
What cares must then attend the toiling swain;
Or when the low'ring spring, with lavish rain,
Beats down the slender stem and bearded grain:
While yet the head is green, or lightly swell'd 425
With milky moisture, overlooks the field.

Ev'n when the farmer, now secure of fear,
Sends in the swains to spoil the finished year:
Ev'n while the reaper fills his greedy hands,
And binds the golden sheaves in brittle bands: 430
Oft have I seen a sudden storm arise,
From all the warring winds that sweep the skies:
The heavy harvest from the root is torn,
And whirl'd aloft the lighter stubble borne;
With such a force the flying rack is driv'n, 435
And such a winter wears the face of heav'n:
And oft whole sheets descend of sluicy rain,
Suck'd by the spongy clouds from off the main:
The lofty skies at once come pouring down,
The promis'd crop and golden labours drown. 440
The dikes are fill'd, and with a roaring sound
The rising rivers float the nether ground;
And rocks the bellowing voice of boiling seas
  rebound.
The Father of the Gods his glory shrouds:
Involv'd in tempests, and a night of clouds, 445
And from the middle darkness flashing out,
By fits he deals his fiery bolts about.
Earth feels the motions of her angry God,
Her entrails tremble, and her mountains nod,
And flying beasts in forests seek abode:

Deep horror seizes ev'ry human breast,
Their pride is humbled, and their fear confess'd;
While he from high his rolling thunder throws,
And fires the mountains with repeated blows:
The rocks are from their old foundations rent; 455
The winds redouble, and the rains augment:
The waves in heaps are dash'd against the shore,
And now the woods, and now the billows roar.

In fear of this, observe the starry signs,
Where Saturn houses, and where Hermes joins.
But first to heav'n thy due devotions pay, 461
And annual gifts on Ceres' altars lay.
When winter's rage abates, when chearful hours
Awake the spring, the spring awakes the flow'rs.
On the green turf thy careless limbs display, 465
And celebrate the mighty mother's day.

For then the hills with pleasing shades are crown'd,
And sleeps are sweeter on the silken ground:
With milder beams the sun securely shines;
Fat are the lambs, and luscious are the wines. 470
Let ev'ry swain adore her pow'r divine,
And milk and honey mix with sparkling wine:
Let all the choir of clowns attend the show,
In long procession, shouting as they go;

Invoking her to blefs their yearly ftores, 475
Inviting plenty to their crouded floors.
Thus in the fpring, and thus in fummer's heat,
Before the fickles touch the ripening wheat,
On Ceres call; and let the lab'ring hind
With oaken wreaths his hollow temples bind: 480
On Ceres let him call, and Ceres praife,
With uncouth dances, and with country lays.

And that by certain figns we may prefage
Of heats and rains, and wind's impetuous rage,
The Sov'reign of the heav'ns has fet on high 485
The moon, to mark the changes of the fky:
When fouthern blafts fhould ceafe, and when the
    fwain
Should near their folds his feeding flocks re—
    ftrain.
For ere the rifing winds begin to roar,
The working feas advance to wafh the fhore: 490
Soft whifpers run along the leafy woods,
And mountains whiftle to the murm'ring floods:
Ev'n then the doubtful billows fcarce abftain
From the tofs'd veffel on the troubled main;
When crying cormorants forfake the fea, 495
And ftretching to the covert wing their way;

When sportful coots run skimming o'er the strand;
When watchful herons leave their wat'ry stand;
And mounting upward with erected flight,
Gain on the skies, and soar above the sight.   500
And oft before tempest'ous winds arise,
The seeming stars fall headlong from the skies;
And, shooting through the darkness, gild the night
With sweeping glories, and long trails of light:
And chaff with eddy winds is whirl'd around,   505
And dancing leaves are lifted from the ground;
And floating feathers on the waters play.
But when the winged thunder takes his way
From the cold north, and east and west engage,
And at their frontiers meet with equal rage.   510
The clouds are crush'd, a glut of gather'd rain
The hollow ditches fills, and floats the plain,
And sailors furl their dropping sheets amain.
Wet weather seldom hurts the most unwise,
So plain the signs, such prophets are the skies: 515
The wary crane foresees it first, and sails
Above the storm, and leaves the lowly vales:
The cow looks up, and from afar can find
The change of heav'n, and snuffs it in the wind,

The swallow skims the river's wat'ry face, 520
The frogs renew the croaks of their loquacious race.
The careful ant her secret cell forsakes,
And drags her eggs along the narrow tracks.
At either horn the rainbow drinks the flood,
Huge flocks of rising rooks forsake their food, 525
And, crying, seek the shelter of the wood.
Besides, the several sorts of wat'ry fowls,
That swim the seas, or haunt the standing pools:
The swans that sail along the silver flood,
And dive with stretching necks to search their food, 530
Then lave their backs with sprinkling dews in vain,
And stem the stream to meet the promis'd rain.
The crow, with clam'rous cries, the show'r demands,
And single stalks along the desart sands.
The nightly virgin, while her wheel she plies, 535
Foresees the storms impending in the skies,
When sparkling lamps their sputt'ring light advance,
And in the sockets oily bubbles dance.

Then after show'rs, 'tis easy to descry
Returning suns, and a serener sky: 540
The stars shine smarter, and the moon adorns,
As with unborrow'd beams, her sharpen'd horns.
The filmy gossimer now flits no more,
Nor halcyons bask on the short sunny shore:
Their litter is not toss'd by sows unclean,   545
But a blue droughty mist descends upon the plain.
And owls, that mark the setting sun, declare
A star-light evening, and a morning fair.
Tow'ring aloft, avenging Nisus flies,
While dar'd below the guilty Scylla lies.   550
Where ever frighted Scylla flies away,
Swift Nisus follows, and pursues his prey.
Where injur'd Nisus takes his airy course,
Thence trembling Scylla flies, and shuns his
   force.
This punishment pursues th' unhappy maid,   555
And thus the purple hair is dearly paid.
Then, thrice the ravens rend the liquid air,
And croaking notes proclaim the settled fair.
Then, round their airy palaces they fly,
To greet the sun: and seiz'd with secret joy,   560

But four nights old, (for that's the surest sign,)
With sharpen'd horns if glorious then she shine;
Next day, not only that, but all the moon,
'Till her revolving race be wholly run,
Are void of tempests, both by land and sea, 585
And sailors in the port their promis'd vows shall pay.
Above the rest, the sun, who never lies,
Foretels the change of weather in the skies:
For if he rise, unwilling, to his race,
Clouds on his brow, and spots upon his face; 590
Or if thro' mists he shoots his sullen beams,
Frugal of light, in loose and straggling streams;
Suspect a drisling day, with southern rain,
Fatal to fruits, and flocks, and promis'd grain.
Or if Aurora, with half-open'd eyes, 595
And a pale sickly cheek, salute the skies;
How shall the vine, with tender leaves, defend
Her teeming clusters, when the storms descend?
When ridgy roofs and tiles can scarce avail
To bar the ruin of the rattling hail. 600
But more than all, the setting sun survey,
When down the steep of heav'n he drives the day.

For oft we find him finishing his race,
With various colours erring on his face;
If fiery red his glowing globe descends,　　605
High winds and furious tempests he portends:
But if his cheeks are swoln with livid blue,
He bodes wet weather by his wat'ry hue;
If dusky spots are varied on his brow,
And streak'd with red, a troubled colour show;　610
That sullen mixture shall at once declare
Winds, rain and storms, and elemental war.
What desp'rate madmen then wou'd venture o'er
The frith, or haul his cables from the shore?
But if with purple rays he brings the light,　　615
And a pure heav'n resigns to quiet night;
No rising winds, or falling storms, are nigh:
But northern breezes through the forest fly,
And drive the rack, and purge the ruffled sky.
Th' unerring sun by certain signs declares,　　620
What the late ev'n, or early morn prepares:
And when the south projects a stormy day,
And when the clearing north will puff the clouds away.

The fun reveals the fecrets of the fky;
And who dares give the fource of light the lye?
The change of empires often he declares,   626
Fierce tumults, hidden treafons, open wars.
He firft the fate of Cæfar did foretel,
And pity'd Rome, when Rome in Cæfar fell.
In iron clouds conceal'd the public light;   630
And impious mortals fear'd eternal night.

  Nor was the fact foretold by him alone:
Nature herfelf ftood forth, and feconded the fun.
Earth, air and feas, with prodigies were fign'd,
And birds obfcene, and howling dogs divin'd.   635
What rocks did Ætna's bellowing mouth expire
From her torn entrails; and what floods of fire!
What clanks were heard, in German fkies afar,
Of arms and armies, rufhing to the war!
Dire earthquakes rent the folid Alps below,   640
And from their fummits fhook th' eternal fnow:
Pale fpectres in the clofe of night were feen,
And voices heard of more than mortal men.
In filent groves, dumb fheep and oxen fpoke,   645
And ftreams ran backward, and their beds for-
    fook:

The yawning earth disclos'd th' abyss of hell;
The weeping statues did the wars foretel;
And holy sweat from brazen idols fell.
Then rising in his might, the king of floods
Rush'd thro' the forest, tore the lofty woods;   650
And rolling onward, with a sweepy sway,
Bore houses, herds, and lab'ring hinds away.
Blood sprang from wells, wolves howl'd in towns
    by night,
And boding victims did the priests affright.
Such peals of thunder never pour'd from high,   655
Nor forky light'ngs flash'd from such a sullen sky.
Red meteors ran across th' ethereal space;
Stars disappear'd, and comets took their place.
For this, th' Emathian plains once more were
    strow'd
With Roman bodies, and just heav'n thought
    good   660
To fatten twice those fields with Roman blood.
Then, after length of time, the lab'ring swains,
Who turn the turfs of those unhappy plains,
Shall rusty piles from the plough'd furrows take,
And over empty helmets pass the rake.   665

Amaz'd at antique titles on the stones,
And mighty relics of gigantic bones.

  Ye home-born deities, of mortal birth!
Thou, father Romulus, and mother Earth,   669
Goddess unmov'd! whose guardian arms extend
O'er Tuscan Tiber's course, and Roman tow'rs
    defend;
With youthful Cæsar your joint pow'rs engage,
Nor hinder him to save the sinking age.
O! let the blood, already spilt, atone
For the past crimes of curs'd Laomedon!   6,5
Heav'n wants thee there; and long the Gods, we
    know,
Have grudg'd thee, Cæsar, to the world below:
Where fraud and rapine, right and wrong con-
    found;
Where impious arms from ev'ry part resound.
And monstrous crimes in ev'ry shape are
    crown'd.   680
The peaceful peasant to the wars is prest;
The fields lie fallow in inglorious rest;
The plain no pasture to the flock affords,
The crooked scythes are straighten'd into swords:

And there Euphrates her soft offspring arms, . 685
And here the Rhine rebellows with alarms;
The neighb'ring cities range on sev'ral sides,
Perfidious Mars long plighted leagues divides,
And o'er the wasted world in triumph rides.
So four fierce coursers starting to the race, 690
Scour thro' the plain, and lengthen ev'ry pace:
Nor rains, nor curbs, nor threat'ning cries they fear,
But force along the trembling charioteer.

VIRGIL's GEORGICS.

GEORGIC II.

THE ARGUMENT.

The subject of the following book is planting. In handling of which argument, the poet shews all the different methods of raising trees: describes their variety; and gives rules for the management of each in particular. He then points out the soils in which the several plants thrive best: and thence takes occasion to run out into the praises of Italy. After which he gives some directions for discovering the nature of every soil; prescribes rules for dressing of vines, olives, &c. And concludes the Georgic with a panegyric on a country life.

THE SECOND BOOK OF THE GEORGICS.

THUS far of tillage, and of heav'nly signs;
Now sing, my Muse, the growth of gen'rous vines:
The shady groves, the woodland progeny,
And the slow product of Minerva's tree.
Great father Bacchus! to my song repair; 5.
For clust'ring grapes are thy peculiar care:
For thee large bunches load the bending vine,
And the last blessings of the year are thine;
To thee his joys the jolly Autumn owes,
When the fermenting juice the vat o'erflows. 10

Come, ſtrip with me, my God, come drench all o'er
Thy limbs in muſt of wine, and drink at ev'ry pore.

  Some trees their birth to bounteous Nature owe;
For ſome, without the pains of planting, grow.
With oſiers thus the banks of brooks abound,   15
Sprung from the wat'ry genius of the ground:
From the ſame principle gray willows come;
Herculean poplar, and the tender broom.
But ſome from ſeeds incloſ'd in earth ariſe;
For thus the maſtful cheſnut mates the ſkies,   20
Hence riſe the branching beech and vocal oak,
Where Jove of old oraculouſly ſpoke.
Some from the root a riſing wood diſcloſe;
Thus elms, and thus the ſavage cherry grows: 24.
Thus the green bays, that binds the poet's brows,
Shoots, and is ſhelter'd by the mother's boughs.

  Theſe ways of planting, Nature did ordain,
For trees and ſhrubs, and all the ſylvan reign.
Others there are, by late experience found;
Some cut the ſhoots, and plant in furrow'd ground;
Some cover rooted ſtalks in deeper mold;   30
Some cloven ſtakes, and (wond'rous to behold,)
Their ſharpen'd ends in earth their footing place,
And the dry poles produce a living race.

Some bow their vines, which bury'd in the plain,
Their tops in diſtant arches riſe again.   35
Others no root require, the lab'rer cuts
Young ſlips, and in the ſoil ſecurely puts.
Ev'n ſtumps of olives, bar'd of leaves, and dead,
Revive, and oft redeem their wither'd head.   40
'Tis uſual now, an inmate graff to ſee
With inſolence invade a foreign tree:.
Thus pears and quinces from the crab-tree come;
And thus the ruddy cornel bears the plum.

 Then let the learned gard'ner mark with care
The kinds of ſtocks, and what thoſe kinds will
  bear,   46
Explore the nature of each ſev'ral tree;
And known, improve with artful induſtry;
And let no ſpot of idle earth be found,
But cultivate the genius of the ground.   50
For open Iſmarus will Bacchus pleaſe;
Taburnus loves the ſhade of olive trees.

 The virtues of the ſev'ral ſoils I ſing.
Mecænas, now thy needful ſuccour bring!
O thou! the better part of my renown,   55
Inſpire thy poet, and thy poem crown;

Embark with me, while I new tracks explore,
With flying sails and breezes from the shore:
Not that my song, in such a scanty space,
So large a subject fully can embrace: 60
Not tho' I were supply'd with iron lungs,
A hundred mouths, fill'd with as many tongues:
But steer my vessel with a steady hand,
And coast along the shore in sight of land.
Nor will I tire thy patience with a train 65
Of preface, or what ancient poets feign.
The trees, which of themselves advance in air,
Are barren kinds, but strongly built and fair:
Because the vigour of the native earth
Maintains the plant, and makes a manly birth. 70
Yet these, receiving graffs of other kind,
Or thence transplanted, change their savage mind;
Their wildness lose, and quitting Nature's part,
Obey the rules and discipline of art.
The same do trees, that, sprung from barren roots
In open fields, transplanted, bear their fruits. 76
For where they grow, the native energy
Turns all into the substance of the tree,
Starves and destroys the fruit, is only made
For brawny bulk, and for a barren shade. 80

The plant that shoots from seed, a sullen tree
At leisure grows, for late posterity;
The gen'rous flavour lost, the fruits decay,
And savage grapes are made the birds ignoble prey.
Much labour is requir'd in trees, to tame   85
Their wild disorder, and in ranks reclaim.
Well must the ground be digg'd, and better dress'd,
New soil to make, and meliorate the rest.
Old stakes of olive trees in plants revive;
By the same methods Paphian myrtles live;   90
But nobler vines by propagation thrive.
From roots hard hazles, and from scyons rise
Tall ash, and taller oak that mates the skies:
Palm, poplar, fir, descending from the steep
Of hills, to try the dangers of the deep.   95
The thin-leav'd arbute, hazle graff's receives,
And planes huge apples bear, that bore but leaves.
Thus mastful beech the bristly chesnut bears,
And the wild ash is white with blooming pears;
And greedy swine from grafted elms are fed   100
With falling acorns, that on oaks are bred.

But various are the ways to change the state
Of plants, to bud, to graff, t' inoculate.

For where the tender rinds of trees disclose
Their shooting gems, a swelling knot there grows;
Just in that space a narrow slit we make, 106.
Then other buds from bearing trees we take;
Inserted thus, the wounded rind we close,
In whose moist womb th' admitted infant grows.
But when the smoother bole from knots is free, 110
We make a deep incision in the tree;
And in the solid wood the slip inclose,
The bat'ning bastard shoots again and grows;
And in short space the laden boughs arise,
With happy fruit advancing to the skies. 115
The mother-plant admires the leaves unknown
Of alien trees, and apples not her own.

Of vegetable woods are various kinds,
And the same species are of sev'ral minds.
Lotes, willows, elms, have different forms allow'd,
So fun'ral cypress rising like a shroud. 121
Fat olive trees of sundry sorts appear,
Of sundry shapes their unctuous berries bear.
Radii long olives, Orchites round produce,
And bitter Pausia pounded for the juice. 125
Alcinous' orchard various apples bears:
Unlike are bergamottes and pounder pears.

Nor our Italian vines produce the shape,
Or taste, or flavour of the Lesbian grape.
The Thasian vines in richer soils abound,   130
The Mereotique grow in barren ground.
The Psythian grape we dry: Legæan juice
Will stamm'ring tongues, and stagg'ring feet produce.
Rathe ripe are some, and some of later kind,
Of golden some, and some of purple rind.   135
How shall I praise the Ræthean grape divine,
Which yet contends not with Falernian wine!
Th' Aminean many a consulship survives,
And longer than the Lydian vintage lives,
Or high Phanæus king of Chian growth: 140
But for large quantities and lasting both,
The less Argitis bears the prize away.
The Rhodian, sacred to the solemn day,
In second services is pour'd to Jove;
And best accepted by the Gods above.   145
Nor must Bumastus his old honours lose,
In length and largeness like the dugs of cows.
I pass the rest, whose ev'ry race and name,
And kinds, are less material to my theme.

Which who wou'd learn, as soon may tell the
    sands,
Driv'n by the western wind on Libyan lands; 150
Or number, when the blust'ring Eurus roars,
The billows beating on Ionian shores.

    Nor ev'ry plant on ev'ry soil will grow:
The sallow loves the wat'ry ground, and low; 155
The marshes, alders; Nature seems t' ordain
The rocky cliff for the wild ash's reign;
The baleful yew to northern blasts assigns;
To shores the myrtles, and to mounts the vines.

    Regard th' extremest cultivated coast, 160
From hot Arabia to the Scythian frost:
All sorts of trees their several countries know;
Black ebon only will in India grow;
And od'rous frankincense on the Sabæan bough.
Balm slowly trickles through the bleeding veins
Of happy shrubs, in Idumæan plains. 165
The green Egyptian thorn, for med'cine good;
With Ethiop's hoary trees and woolly wood,
Let others tell: and how the Ceres spin
Their fleecy forests in a slender twine. 170
With mighty trunks of trees on Indian shores,
Whose height above the feather'd arrow soars,

Shot from the toughest bough; and by the brawn
Of expert archers, with vast vigour drawn.
Sharp-tasted citrons Median climes produce; 175
Bitter the rind, but gen'rous is the juice:
A cordial fruit, a present antidote
Against the direful stepdame's deadly draught:
Who, mixing wicked weeds with words impure,
The fate of envy'd orphans would procure. 180
Large is the plant, and like a laurel grows,
And did it not a diff'rent scent disclose,
A laurel were: the fragrant flow'rs contemn
The stormy winds, tenacious of their stem.
With this the Medes, to lab'ring age bequeath 185
New lungs, and cure the sourness of the breath.

But neither Median woods, (a plenteous land),
Fair Ganges, Hermus rolling golden sand,
Nor Bactria, nor the richer Indian fields,
Nor all the gummy stores Arabia yields; 190
Nor any foreign earth of greater name,
Can with sweet Italy contend in fame.
No bulls whose nostrils breathe a living flame
Have turn'd our turf; no teeth of serpents here
Were sown, an armed host, and iron crop to bear.

But fruitful vines, and the fat olives freight, 196
And harvest heavy with their fruitful weight,
Adorn our fields; and on the chearful green,
The grazing flocks and lowing herds are seen.
The warrior horse here bred, is taught to train: 200
There flows Clitumnus thro' the flow'ry plain;
Whose waves, for triumphs after prosp'rous war,
The victim ox, and snowy sheep prepare.
Perpetual spring our happy climate sees;
Twice breed the cattle, and twice bear the trees;
And summer suns recede by slow degrees. 206

 Our land is from the rage of tigers freed,
Nor nourishes the lion's angry seed;
Nor pois'nous aconite is here produc'd,
Or grows unknown, or is, when known, refus'd.
Nor in so vast a length our serpents glide, 211
Or rais'd on such a spiry volume ride.

 Next add our cities of illustrious name,
Their costly labour, and stupendous frame:
Our forts on steepy hills, that far below 215
See wanton streams, in winding vallies flow.
Our two-fold seas, that washing either side,
A rich recruit of foreign stores provide.

Our spacious lakes; thee, Larius, first; and next
Benacus, with tempest'ous billows vext.   220
Or shall I praise thy ports, or mention make
Of the vast mound that binds the Lucrine lake?
Or the disdainful sea, that, shut from thence,
Roars round the structure, and invades the fence.
There, where secure, the Julian waters glide,   225
Or where Avernus' jaws admit the Tyrrhene tide.
Our quarries, deep in earth, were fam'd of old
For veins of silver, and for ore of gold.
Th' inhabitants themselves, their country grace;
Hence rose the Marsian and Sabellian race: 230
Strong-limb'd and stout, and to the wars inclin'd;
And hard Ligurians, a laborious kind:
And Volscians arm'd with iron-headed darts,
Besides an offspring of undaunted hearts,
The Decii, Marii, great Camillus came   235
From hence, and greater Scipio's double name:
And mighty Cæsar, whose victorious arms
To farthest Asia carry fierce alarms:
Avert unwarlike Indians from his Rome;
Triumph abroad, secure our peace at home,   240

Hail, sweet Saturnian soil! of fruitful grain
Great Parent, greater of illustrious men,
For thee my tuneful accents will I raise,
And treat of arts disclos'd in ancient days:
Once more unlock for thee the sacred spring,   245.
And old Ascræan verse in Roman cities sing.

The nature of their sev'ral soils now see;
Their strength, their colour, their fertility;
And first for heath and barren hilly ground,
Where meagre clay and flinty stones abound;   250
Where the poor soil all succour seems to want,
Yet this suffices the Palladian plant.
Undoubted signs of such a soil are found,
For here wild olive shoots o'erspread the ground,
And heaps of berries strew the fields around.   255.
But where the soil, with fatt'ning moisture fill'd,
Is cloath'd with grass, and fruitful to be till'd;
Such as in chearful vales we view from high;
Which dripping rocks with rolling streams supply,
And feed with ooze, where rising hillocks run   260
In length, and open to the southern sun;
Where fern succeeds, ungrateful to the plow,
That gentle ground to gen'rous grapes allow,

Strong stocks of vines it will in time produce,
And overflow the vats with friendly juice. 265
Such as our priests in golden goblets pour
To Gods, the givers of the chearful hour.
Then when the bloated Thuscan blows his horn,
And reeking entrails are in chargers borne.

If herds or fleecy flocks be more thy care, 270
Or goats that graze the field, and burn it bare;
Then seek Tarentum's lawns, and farthest coast,
Or such a field as hapless Mantua lost:
Where silver swans sail down the wat'ry road,
And graze the floating herbage of the flood, 275
There chrystal streams perpetual tenour keep,
Nor food nor springs are wanting to thy sheep.
For what the day devours, the nightly dew
Shall to the morn in pearly drops renew.
Fat crumbling earth is fitter for the plow, 280
Putrid and loose above, and black below;
For ploughing is an imitative toil,
Resembling nature in an easy soil.
No land for seed like this, no fields afford
So large an income to the village lord! 285
No toiling teams from harvest-labour come
So late at night, so heavy laden home,

The like of forest land is understood,
From whence the surly ploughman grubs the wood,
Which had for length of ages idle stood. 290
Then birds forsake the ruins of their seat,
And flying from their nests their callow young forget.
The coarse lean gravel on the mountain sides,
Scarce dewy bev'rage for the bees provides: 294
Nor chalk nor crumbling stones, the food of snakes,
That work in hollow earth their winding tracks.
The soil exhaling clouds of subtile dews,
Imbibing moisture which with ease she spews;
Which rusts not iron, and whose mold is clean;
Well cloath'd with chearful grass and ever-green,
Is good for olives, and aspiring vines, 301
Embracing husband elms, in am'rous twines:
Is fit for feeding cattle, fit to sow,
And equal to the pasture and the plow.
 Such is the soil of fat Campanian fields, 305
Such large increase the land that joins Vesuvius yields,
And such a country could Acerra boast,
Till Clanius overflow'd th' unhappy coast.

I teach thee next the diff'ring soils to know;
The light for vines, the heavier for the plow. 310
Chuse first a place for such a purpose fit,
There dig the solid earth, and sink a pit.
Next fill the hole with its own earth again,
And trample with thy feet, and tread it in;
Then if it rise not to the former height 315
Of superfice, conclude that soil is light:
A proper ground for pasturage and vines.
But if the sullen earth, so press'd, repines,
Within its native mansion to retire,
And stays without, a heap of heavy mire; 320
'Tis good for arable, a glebe that asks
Tough teams of oxen, and laborious tasks.

Salt earth and bitter are not fit to sow,
Nor will be tam'd and mended by the plow. 324
Sweet grapes degen'rate there, and fruits declin'd
From their first flav'rous taste, renounce their kind.
This truth by sure experiment is try'd:
For first an osier colander provide
Of twigs thick wrought, (such toiling peasants
  twine, 329
When thro' strait passages they strain their wine;)

In this close vessel place that earth accurs'd, 331
But fill'd brimful with wholesome water first:
Then run it through, the drops will rope around,
And by the bitter taste disclose the ground.
The fatter earth by handling we may find. 335
With ease distinguish'd from the meagre kind:
Poor soil will crumble into dust, the rich
Will to the fingers cleave like clammy pitch.
Moist earth produces corn and grass, but both
Too rank and too luxuriant in their growth. 340
Let not my land so large a promise boast,
Lest the lank ears in length of stem be lost.
The heavier earth is by her weight betray'd,
The lighter in the poising hand is weigh'd:
'Tis easy to distinguish by the sight, 345
The colour of the soil, and black from white.
But the cold ground is difficult to know,
Yet this the plants that prosper there will show;
Black ivy, pitch-trees, and the baleful yew.
These rules consider'd well, with early care 350
The vineyard destin'd for thy vines prepare:
But, long before the planting, dig the ground,
With furrows deep that cast a rising mound:
The clods, expos'd to winter winds, will bake;
For putrid earth will best in vineyards take, 355

And hoary frosts, after the painful toil
Of delving hinds, will rot the mellow soil.

Some peasants, not t' omit the nicest care,
Of the same soil their nursery prepare,
With that of their plantation; lest the tree 360
Tranflated, should not with the foil agree.
Beside, to plant it as it was, they mark
The heav'n's four quarters on the tender bark;
And to the north or south restore the side,
Which at their birth did heat or cold abide. 365
So strong is custom, such effects can use
In tender souls of pliant plants produce.

Chuse next a province for thy vineyard's reign,
On hills above, or in the lowly plain:
If fertile fields or vallies be thy choice, 370
Plant thick, for bounteous Bacchus will rejoice
In close plantations there. But if the vine
On rising ground be plac'd, or hills supine,
Extend thy loose battalions largely wide,
Opening thy ranks and files on either side: 375
But marshall'd all in order as they stand,
And let no soldier straggle from his band.
As legions in the field their front display,
To try the fortune of some doubtful day,

And move to meet their foes with sober pace, 380
Strict to their figure, tho' in wider space;
Before the battle joins; while from afar
The field yet glitters with the pomp of war,
And equal Mars like an imperial lord,
Leaves all to fortune and the dint of sword; 385
So let thy vines in intervals be set,
But not their rural discipline forget:
Indulge their width, and add a roomy space,
That their extremest lines may scarce embrace;
Nor this alone t' indulge a vain delight, 390
And make a pleasing prospect for the sight:
But for the ground itself, this only way
Can equal vigour to the plants convey;
Which crouded, want the room their branches to display.

How deep they must be planted, would'st thou know? 395
In shallow furrows vines securely grow.
Not so the rest of plants; for Jove's own tree,
That holds the woods in awful sov'reignty,
Requires a depth of lodging in the ground;
And, next the lower skies, a bed profound: 400

High as his topmoſt boughs to heav'n aſcend,
So low his roots to hell's dominion tend.
Therefore, nor winds nor winter's rage o'erthrows
His bulky body, but unmov'd he grows.
For length of ages laſts his happy reign,   405
And lives of mortal men contend in vain.
Full in the midſt of his own ſtrength he ſtands,
Stretching his brawny arms, and leafy hands;
His ſhade protects the plains, his head the hills commands.

   The hurtful hazle in the vineyard ſhun;   410
Nor plant it to receive the ſetting ſun:
Nor break the topmoſt branches from the tree;
Nor prune, with blunted knife, the progeny.
Root up wild olives from thy labour'd lands:
For ſparkling fire, from hinds unwary hands,   415
Is often ſcatter'd o'er their unctuous rinds,
And after ſpread abroad by raging winds.
For firſt the ſmouldring flame the trunk receives,
Aſcending thence, it crackles in the leaves;
At length victorious to the top aſpires,   420
Involving all the wood in ſmoky fires,
But moſt, when driv'n by winds, the flaming ſtorm
Of the long files deſtroys the beauteous form.

In ashes then th' unhappy vineyard lies,
Nor will the blasted plants from ruin rise;   425
Nor will the wither'd stock be green again,
But the wild olive shoots, and shades th' ungrateful plain.
Be not seduc'd with wisdom's empty shows,
To stir the peaceful ground when Boreas blows.
When winter frosts constrain the field with cold,
The fainty root can take no steady hold.   431
But when the golden spring reveals the year,
And the white bird returns, whom serpents fear;
That season deem the best to plant thy vines,
Next that, is when autumnal warmth declines;   435
Ere heat is quite decay'd, or cold begun,
Or Capricorn admits the winter sun.

 The spring adorns the woods, renews the leaves,
The womb of earth the genial seed receives.
For then Almighty Jove descends, and pours   440
Into his buxom bride his fruitful show'rs;
And mixing his large limbs with hers, he feeds
Her birth with kindly juice, and fosters teeming seeds.
Then joyous birds frequent the lonely grove,
And beasts, by nature stung, renew their love.   445

Then fields the blades of bury'd corn disclose,
And while the balmy western spirit blows,
Earth to the breath her bosom dares expose.
With kindly moisture then the plants abound,
The grass securely springs above the ground; 450
The tender twig shoots upward to the skies,
And on the faith of the new sun relies.
The swerving vines on the tall elms prevail,
Unhurt by southern show'rs or northern hail.
They spread their gems the genial warmth to share,
And boldly trust the buds in open air. 456
In this soft season (let me dare to sing)
The world was hatch'd by heav'n's imperial king:
In prime of all the year, and holy-days of spring.
Then did the new creation first appear;
Nor other was the tenour of the year:
When laughing heav'n did the great birth attend,
And eastern winds their wintry breath suspend;
Then sheep first saw the sun in open fields,
And savage beasts were sent to stock the wilds; 465
And golden stars flew up to light the skies,
And man's relentless race, from stony quarries rise.
Nor cou'd the tender, new creation, bear
Th' excessive heats or coldness of the year;

But chill'd by winter, or by summer fir'd, 470
The middle temper of the spring requir'd.
When warmth and moisture did at once abound,
And heav'n's indulgence brooded on the ground.

For what remains in depth of earth secure
Thy cover'd plants, and dung with hot manure;
And shells and gravel in the ground inclose; 476
For thro' their hollow chinks the water flows:
Which, thus imbib'd, returns in misty dews,
And steaming up, the rising plant renews.
Some husbandmen, of late, have found the way,
A hilly heap of stones above to lay, 481
And press the plants with shreds of potters clay.
This fence against immod'rate rains they found;
Or when the Dog-star cleaves the thirsty ground.
Be mindful when thou hast intomb'd the shoot, 485
With store of earth around to feed the root;
With iron teeth of rakes and prongs to move
The crusted earth, and loosen it above.
Then exercise thy sturdy steers to plough
Betwixt thy vines, and teach the feeble row 490
To mount on reeds, and wands, and, upward led,
On ashen poles to raise their forky head.

On these new crutches let them learn to walk,
Till swerving upwards, with a stronger stalk,
They brave the winds, and clinging to their guide,
On tops of elms at length triumphant ride.   496
But in their tender nonage, while they spread
Their springing leaves, and lift their infant head,
And upward while they shoot in open air,
Indulge their childhood, and the nurseling spare.
Nor exercise thy rage on new-born life,   501
But let thy hand supply the pruning-knife;
And crop luxuriant stragglers, nor be loth
To strip the branches of their leafy growth:
But when the rooted vines, with steady hold, 505
Can clasp their elms, then husbandman be bold
To lop the disobedient boughs, that stray'd
Beyond their ranks: let crooked steel invade
The lawless troops, which discipline disclaim,
And their superfluous growth with rigour tame. 510
Next, fenc'd with hedges and deep ridges round,
Exclude th' incroaching cattle from thy ground,
While yet the tender gems but just appear,
Unable to sustain th' uncertain year;
Whose leaves are not alone foul winter's prey, 515
But oft by summer suns are scorch'd away;

And worfe than both, become th' unworthy
    browfe,
Of buffaloes, falt goats, and hungry cows,
For not December's froft that burns the bows,
Nor Dog-days parching heat that fplits the rocks,
Are half fo harmful as the greedy flocks;   521
Their venom'd bite, and fcars indented on the
    flocks.
For this the malefactor goat was laid
On Bacchus' altar, and his forfeit paid.
At Athens thus old comedy began,   525
When round the ftreets the reeling actors ran;
In country villages and crofling ways,
Contending for the prizes of their plays:
And glad, with Bacchus, on the graffy foil,
Leap'd o'er the fkins of goats befmear'd with oil. 530
Thus Roman youth deriv'd from ruin'd Troy,
In rude Saturnian rhymes exprefs their joy:
With taunts, and laughter loud, their audience pleafe,
Deform'd with vizards, cut from barks of trees:
In jolly hymns they praife the God of wine,
Whofe earthen images adorn the pine;   536
And there are hung on high, in honour of the
    vine:

A madness so devout the vineyard fills,
In hollow vallies and on rising hills;
On whate'er side he turns his honest face, 540
And dances in the wind, those fields are in his grace.
To Bacchus, therefore, let us tune our lays,
And in our mother-tongue resound his praise.
Thin cakes in chargers, and a guilty goat,
Dragg'd by the horns, be to his altars brought; 545
Whose offer'd entrails shall his crime reproach,
And drip their fatness from the hazle broach.
To dress thy vines new labour is requir'd,
Nor must the painful husbandman be tir'd:
For thrice, at least, in compass of a year, 550
Thy vineyard must employ the sturdy steer,
To turn the glebe; besides thy daily pain
To break the clods, and make the surface plain;
T' unload the branches, or the leaves to thin,
That suck the vital moisture of the vine. 555
Thus in a circle runs the peasant's pain,
And the year rolls within itself again.
Ev'n in the lowest months when storms have shed
From vines the hairy honours of their head,
Not then the drudging hind his labour ends, 560
But to the coming year his care extends;

Ev'n then the naked vine he persecutes;
His pruning-knife at once reforms and cuts.
Be first to dig the ground, be first to burn
The branches lopt, and first the props return   565
Into thy house, that bore the burden'd vines;
But last to reap the vintage of thy wines.
Twice in the year luxuriant leaves o'ershade
Th' incumber'd vine; rough brambles twice invade;
Hard labour both! commend the large excess   570
Of spacious vineyards; cultivate the less.
Besides, in woods the shrubs of prickly thorn,
Sallows and reeds, on banks of rivers born.
Remain to cut; for vineyards useful found,   574
To stay thy vines, and fence thy fruitful ground:
Nor when thy tender trees at length are bound;
When peaceful vines from pruning-hooks are free,
When husbands have survey'd the last degree,
And utmost files of plants, and order'd ev'ry tree;
Ev'n when they sing at ease in full content,   580
Insulting o'er the toils they underwent;
Yet still they find a future task remain,
To turn the soil and break the clods again:
And after all, their joys are unsincere,
While falling rains on ripening grapes they fear.

Quite opposite to these are olives found, 586
No dressing they require, and dread no wound;
No rakes nor harrows need, but fix'd below,
Rejoice in open air, and unconcern'dly grow.
The soil itself due nourishment supplies: 590
Plough but the furrows, and the fruits arise:
Content with small endeavours till they spring.
Soft peace they figure, and sweet plenty bring;
Then olives plant, and hymns to Pallas sing.

Thus apple-trees, whose trunks are strong to bear,
Their spreading boughs exert themselves in air;
Want no supply, but stand secure alone, 597
Nor trusting foreign forces but their own,
Till with the ruddy freight the bending branches groan.

Thus trees of nature, and each common bush
Uncultivated thrive, and with red berries blush, 601
Vile shrubs are shorn for browse: the tow'ring height
Of unctuous trees are torches for the night.
And shall we doubt (indulging easy sloth)
To sow, to set, and to reform their growth? 605
To leave the lofty plants; the lowly kind
Are for the shepherd or the sheep design'd.

Ev'n humble broom and osiers have their use,
And shade for sheep and food for flocks produce;
Hedges for corn, and honey for the bees;   610
Besides the pleasing prospect of the trees.
How goodly looks Cytorus, ever green
With boxen groves, with what delight are seen
Narycian woods of pitch, whose gloomy shade
Seems for retreat of heav'nly Muses made!   615
But much more pleasing are those fields to see,
That need not plows nor human industry.
Ev'n cold Caucasean rocks with trees are spread,
And wear green forests on their hilly head.
Tho' bending from the blast of eastern storms,   620
Tho' shent their leaves, and shatter'd are their arms;
Yet heav'n their various plants for use designs:
For houses cedars, and for shipping pines.
Cypress provides for spokes, and wheels of wains
And all for keels of ships, that scour the wat'ry
    plains.   625
Willows in twigs are fruitful, elms in leaves;
The war from stubborn myrtle shafts receives;
From cornels jav'lins; and the tougher yew
Receives the bending figure of a bow.   629

Nor box, nor limes, without their use are made,
Smooth grain'd, and proper for the turner's trade;
Which curious hands may carve, and steel with
    ease invade.
Light alder stems the Po's impetuous tide,
And bees in hollow oaks their honey hide.
Now balance, with these gifts the fumy joys   635
Of wine, attended with eternal noise.
Wine urg'd to lawless lust the Centaurs train,
Thro' wine they quarrel'd, and thro' wine were
    slain.

  O happy, if he knew his happy state!
The swain, who, free from business and debate,
Receives his easy food from Nature's hand,   641
And just returns of cultivated land!
No palace, with a lofty gate, he wants,
T' admit the tides of early visitants,
With eager eyes devouring as they pass,   645
The breathing figures of Corinthian brass.
No statues threaten from high pedestals;
No Persian arras hides his homely walls,
With antic vests; which, thro' their shady fold,
Betray the streaks of ill-dissembled gold.   650

He boasts no wool, whose native white is dy'd
With purple poison of Assyrian pride.
No costly drugs of Araby defile,
With foreign scents the sweetness of his oil.
But easy quiet, a secure retreat,   655.
A harmless life that knows not how to cheat,
With home-bred plenty the rich owner bless,
And rural pleasures crown his happiness.
Unvex'd with quarrels, undisturb'd with noise,
The country king his peaceful realm enjoys: 660
Cool grots and living lakes, the flow'ry pride
Of meads, and streams that thro' the valley glide;
And shady groves that easy sleep invite,
And after toilsome days, a soft repose at night.
Wild beasts of nature in his woods abound;   665
And youth, of labour patient, plough the ground;
Inur'd to hardship and to homely fare,
Nor venerable age is wanting there,
In great examples to the youthful train:
Nor are the Gods ador'd with rites profane.   670
From hence Astrea took her flight, and here
The prints of her departing steps appear.

   Ye sacred Muses, with whose beauty fir'd,
My soul is ravish'd, and my train inspir'd;

Whose priest I am, whose holy fillets wear, 675
Wou'd you your poet's first petition hear;
Give me the ways of wand'ring stars to know;
The depths of heav'n above, and earth below.
Teach me the various labours of the moon,
And whence proceed th' eclipses of the sun. 680
Why flowing tides prevail upon the main,
And in what dark recess they shrink again.
What shakes the solid earth; what cause delays
The summer nights, and shortens winter days.
But if my heavy blood restrain the flight 685
Of my free soul, aspiring to the height
Of nature and unclouded fields of light,
My next desire is, void of care and strife,
To lead a soft, secure, inglorious life.
A country cottage near a chrystal flood, 690
A winding valley, and a lofty wood.
Some God conduct me to the sacred shades,
Where bacchanals are sung by Spartan maids,
Or lift me high to Hæmus' hilly crown,
Or in the plains of Tempe lay me down; 695
Or lead me to some solitary place,
And cover my retreat from human race.

Happy the man, who, studying Nature's laws,
Thro' known effects can trace the secret cause.
His mind possessing in a quiet state, 700
Fearless of Fortune, and resign'd to Fate.
And happy too is he, who decks the bow'rs
Of sylvans, and adores the rural pow'rs;
Whose mind, unmov'd, the bribes of courts can see,
Their glitt'ring baits, and purple slavery. 705
Nor hopes the people's praise, nor fears their frown,
Nor, when contending kindred tear the crown,
Well set up one, or pull another down.

Without concern he hears, but hears from far,
Of tumults, and descents, and distant war: 710
Nor with a superstitious fear is aw'd,
For what befals at home, or what abroad.
Nor envies he the rich their happy store,
Nor his own peace disturbs, with pity for the poor.
He feeds on fruits, which, of their own accord, 715
The willing ground and laden trees afford.
From his lov'd home no lucre him can draw;
The senate's mad decrees he never saw,
Nor heard, at bawling bars, corrupted law.

Some to the seas, and some to camps resort, 720
And some with impudence invade the court.
In foreign countries others seek renown;
With wars and taxes others waste their own,
And houses burn, and houshold Gods deface, 724
To drink in bowls which glitt'ring gems enchase;
To loll on couches, rich with Cytron steds,
And lay their guilty limbs in Tyrian beds,
This wretch in earth intombs his golden ore,
Hov'ring and brooding on his bury'd store.
Some patriot fools to popular praise aspire, 730
Of public speeches, which worse fools admire.
While from both benches, with redoubl'd sounds,
Th' applause of lords and commoners abounds.
Some thro' ambition, or thro' thirst of gold,
Have slain their brothers, or their country sold; 735
And leaving their sweet homes, in exile run
To lands that lie beneath another sun.

The peasant, innocent of all these ills,
With crooked ploughs the fertile fallows tills;
And the round year with daily labour fills. 740
And hence the country markets are supply'd;
Enough remains for houshold charge beside;

His wife and tender children to sustain,
And gratefully to feed his dumb deserving train.
Nor cease his labours, till the yellow field   745
A full return of bearded harvest yields;
A crop so plenteous, as the land to load,
O'ercome the crouded barns, and lodge on ricks
    abroad.
Thus ev'ry sev'ral season is employ'd:
Some spent in toil, and some in ease enjoy'd.   750
The yeaning ewes prevent the springing year;
The laded boughs their fruits in autumn bear:
'Tis then the vine her liquid harvest yields,
Bak'd in the sun-shine of ascending fields.
The winter comes, and then the falling mast,   755
For greedy swine provides a full repast.
Then olives, ground in mills, their fatness boast,
And winter fruits are mellow'd by the frost.
His cares are eas'd with intervals of bliss;
His little children climbing for a kiss,   760
Welcome their father's late return at night;
His faithful bed is crown'd with chaste delight.
His kine with swelling udders ready stand,
And, lowing for the pail, invite the milker's hand.

His wanton kids, with budding horns prepar'd 765
Fight harmless battles in his homely yard;
Himself in rustic pomp, on holidays,
To rural pow'rs a just oblation pays,
And on the green his careless limbs displays.
The hearth is in the midst; the herdsmen round
The chearful fire, provoke his health in goblets
    crown'd. 771
He calls on Bacchus, and propounds the prize;
The groom his fellow-groom at buts defies;
And bends his bow, and levels with his eyes.
Or stripp'd for wrestling, smears his limbs with oil,
And watches with a trip his foe to foil. 776
Such was the life the frugal Sabines led;
So Remus and his brother God were bred:
From whom th' austere Etrurian virtue rose·
And this rude life our homely fathers chose. 780
Old Rome from such a race deriv'd her birth,
(The seat of empire, and the conquer'd earth;)
Which now on seven high hills triumphant reigns,
And in that compass all the world contains.
Ere Saturn's rebel son usurp'd the skies, 785
When beasts were only slain for sacrifice;

While peaceful Crete enjoy'd her ancient lord,
Ere founding hammers forg'd th' inhuman sword:
Ere hollow drums were beat, before the breath
Of brazen trumpets rung the peals of death; 790
The good old God his hunger did affwage
With roots and herbs, and gave the golden age,
But over-labour'd with fo long a courfe,
'Tis time to fet at eafe the fmoaking horfe.

END OF THE FIRST VOLUME.

www.ingramcontent.com/pod-product-compliance
Lightning Source LLC
Chambersburg PA
CBHW021204230426
43667CB00006B/552